CAPTAIN BIONIC

To Lt. Tony George IRT
and all of the First Responders of America,
and foremost to my son Luis Cumba Jr.,
who gave a part of his body to save my life.

Published by Mindstir Media, LLC
45 Lafayette Rd | Suite 181| North Hampton, NH 03862 | USA
1.800.767.0531 | www.mindstirmedia.com

Printed in the United States of America
ISBN-13: 978-0-9600881-1-9
Library of Congress Control Number: 2019900807

CAPTAIN BIONIC

The Amazing Luis Cumba Story

of First Responders:
America's Everyday Heroes

LUIS CUMBA
with Dana Dorfman

MINDSTIR MEDIA

TABLE OF CONTENTS

ABOUT AUTHOR LUIS CUMBA

By Dana Dorfman

Luis Cumba's book rocks!

It will leave a deep, powerful and lasting impression on all who read it. While Luis has always had an appetite for living and learning, I believe he found great pleasure in writing his story. When Luis spoke to me about his death it came out of the blue. I wasn't expecting it and I must admit that I was simply mesmerized. Later, he would tell me about the message he received.

Luis Cumba grew up doing tasks with his pop. He loved working alongside his father. Sometimes, they would work for hours not exchanging so much as a word, but he loved every minute of it. He was proud that his dad took him under his wing and made sure he was consistently employed and accumulating new experiences and picking up new skills. Luis learned a lot about safety working with his old man which he valued in his career as a police officer. Luis learned to cook, clean and fix almost anything. He had jobs from pumping gas to working in restaurants.

During his middle school years his father had a business working as an Operating Engineer. He bought a carting company and the family learned later that it was purchased from a Mafia capo. Luis used to get up at 3am and pick up cans to earn money while his uncle drove the truck. They would scour areas for discarded bottles and cans for redemption. He became physically strong as a result. He walked to middle school where he wrestled and played lacrosse. He also protected classmates in the event they were picked on. No one wanted to deal with Luis, because of his toughness, which continues today.

Luis went to high school and easily scored high in his honor classes. He could solve mathematical and real-world problems easily and was always able to move on to his next set of skills on any subject. He loved history. He remembered everything he learned! Luis knew there was no failing at anything. He was able to challenge the way teachers and students thought from government to physical education. Not only did Luis excel as a great athlete, he emerged as a recognized scholar at seventeen years of age. Luis continued to protect the weak in all grades. Upon graduating, he grew up quick and got a job at one of the largest mental institutions in Cleveland, working with the mentally challenged. He also started to work a second job as a mechanic, made a great income and bought a fancy '98 gold Olds that resembled a Cadillac, but I will let him fill you in on the Cadillac story!

Luis Cumba is a knock out! Luis is the type of guy that can pull up a chair next to you and just start talking, and immediately you feel an instant friendship with him! This is Luis Cumba. This is what Luis is all about. I admire him wanting to talk about his death as it was such an amazing part of his life. Soaring to the top of his law enforcement career, he managed to successfully juggle his academia with high grades and shape the course of his life with wisdom and pride. There is so much to Luis Cumba. His interests are many.

Luis Cumba and his family came to the U.S. Mainland from Puerto Rico when he was just about three years old. He is a Puerto Rican American, a Retired Firefighter and Wildfire Expert and a Police Captain from the beautiful city of Cleveland, Ohio. He is a Civil Rights Expert, a First Responder and an expert in Civil Rights Disaster, Riot Control, Civil Disorder, Homeland Security, Internal Affairs Investigation, Police Brutality and a Special Weapons and Tactics (SWAT) Command Specialist where he led the rescue in 2007 of 450 students and staff who were being shot at in a school shooting in Cleveland. Luis has studied every major incident around the country from school shootings to kidnappings to learn and build the best SWAT team in Cleveland and throughout the USA. His focus was always on using the finest equipment and saving lives.

The first movie Luis ever saw in a movie theater was *The Ten Commandments*. He loved it! It was an evening in Philly that he will never forget. Dynamic and fascinating, he remembers he went with his cousins to see the movie with his blood pumping! He was so excited!

It was the first time any of them had been to the big screen! Luis remembers how he stayed in his seat, long after the movie was over to read the credits. He didn't want to leave. *The Ten Commandments* remains his favorite movie of all time.

It is not often I assist someone write a book about their life and death. It is not often when readers get to read about someone who has died, and they can tell you about it! Luis Cumba's book is fascinating. He is an amazing man with a strong tie to God. I personally love his spirit, his sense of humor and admire his stamina and feel his good karma! I am impressed with his accomplishments as well as his life and death! But more importantly, I am very touched by who Luis Cumba is. He is a sensitive man who tells it like it is.

It has been my honor to assist Luis with the writing of his story.

And now, it is my honor to present Luis Cumba.

You are going to love him!

Dear Reader,

Do you know that I wasn't raised on TV?

Can you imagine not having a TV around while growing up? It wouldn't be until I was about twenty-five years old or so that I would be able to come home, plop down on the sofa and flip on the television. Now, I will tell you that my childhood was just fine without TV. I've never been bored a single day in my life. I was always doing something. I got to know myself instead of hanging around a TV set and to this day I don't feel a need to turn on the set to unwind or be entertained. Furthermore, I think this is the reason I am so creative in my life, and such an avid reader.

I have had a voracious appetite for learning from a very young age. I always had different strategies for gaining knowledge. Whether I was learning from my dad about how to be a great mechanic or I was being taught from a teacher at school or I was reading on my own, learning went well beyond the classroom or the person teaching me. Every kind of learning is important to grow in the world. I have, since I can remember, had a creative vision for myself and wrestled often with my creative spirit. I have found it interesting that in the times of dissention and turmoil that my creative spirit has contributed to improving intercultural understanding and promoting social justice in the communities I frequented as a police officer. I think my creative spirit allowed me to be supportive and inspiring in all my roles in law enforcement. I was committed to inspiring women and minorities and encouraging all to move through the ranks of law enforcement.

I was always comfortable being myself, except I must admit I was rather shy. I knew my beliefs right away. I can tell you I always tried to be kind, good to others and always see the good in someone else.

I believe I am a perfectionist striving to be better which you will see really comes forth in my pages. I do think I experienced a certain flavor of joy that comes with relying on yourself to be amused. I learned a lot about my personality and sense of humor and learned to appreciate my drive for success. I think my gold Olds was an interesting part of my life for so many reasons and I still think it could have made an interesting episode on TV! That gold Olds could have been a Hollywood icon!

I want to take this opportunity to welcome everyone to my pages! Writing this book has been a stroll down memory lane for me and has been a lot of fun but I don't think I have ever worked so hard to do something! It is one thing to live your life, but to write about it is entirely something else! It isn't easy to write about your life and death. God brought me back and it has been well worth writing about. Pulling this book together has been a bit challenging at times because there is so much to me. If you find that I hop around a bit, repeat something here and there or just tell you how much I love God a couple of times in this book, it is just who I am.

I'm not sure if I was born this brave soul or some super hero, but I was the one who always turned the lights on in the house to make sure that my family was okay. I was this richly eclectic brew of courage filled with a blend of soul, Sinatra, sophisticated Broadway, jazz, blues, rock and roll, funk and lots and lots of Latin moves and soul and salsa! I refused to confine myself to any one sound or musical style. I would dance my heart out to anything and still do! I always made a dance floor sparkle. I lit it up and made the audience swoon. I sing and dance and entrance! I always have, and always will! Maybe I don't shake it up and move as fast as I did, but I've still got the moves!

When I sing and dance I forge on into my own form of expression. I'm really a one-man band. I play the bass and make any stage shake! I have a love for soft sentimental ballads, tender love songs and simple Tony Bennett and Sinatra music and I love complex arrangements also. I like Motown and Marvin Gaye and Ray Charles and Stevie Wonder, Duke Ellington and the Shoo-Be-Do-Be-Do Stuff! I like rhythm and I was born with rhythm high on top of a beautiful mountain in Cayey, Puerto Rico. That mountain was so high it seemed as if I could touch God! I was born with Latin blood that won't quit and a spirit that won't stop. I love life! What can I say! And I want you to know that my death has really put a new spin on my life, but I will be getting to that.

I never ignored the person next to me growing up if they needed help. They could be a stranger or a friend or family. I always tried to protect the lady or man who was being victimized by the thug destroying himself to steal a stranger's gold watch. I couldn't make sense out of stealing. If you wanted money you worked for it. Don't go off grumbling about not having something and stealing. Go out and get a job and work for it. And getting a job didn't mean dozing behind the counter. If it was an odd job or grabbing a paint brush and giving something a couple of coats of paint, you worked your butt off. If you were sitting behind a desk or getting your hands dirty and working, you worked to get what you wanted. That was the Cumba way. My dad always had a job. I never remember him just sitting around the house. It was a form of personal and professional discipline with the Cumba's. All my brothers and sisters worked hard to get what they wanted.

I believe I have been a protective type of a person ever since I was born. Being protective has been my mantra. As a little boy, I was playful with my mother and had a boyish frankness with my dad and always was tender and protective with my sisters and stood up for my brothers. I understood the fear and pain that bullies inflicted upon others and I didn't like that. Bullies didn't stand a chance when I was around, and they knew it. I also admired first responders from such a young age and wanted to be part of their rescue spirit. I admired their courage and heroics and I wanted to be just like them. I admired they way they went out in blizzards to rescue someone or save an animal or help in some way. I pictured the First Responders like a protective shield. I admired them and as I grew up I realized my nature was filled with safeguarding tendencies. It is not a surprise that I grew up to protect human beings and animals from harm and injury. I was born with a heroic nature and it has stayed with me to this day and so it is no wonder that I would grow up to be a first responder.

I never was friends with anyone who had a brute nature about them.

I had nothing in common with those bullying types. I didn't find them interesting, I found them revolting. The sub-human brute looms large in Hollywood films but unfortunately looms large in real life as well. Scenes in combat, drug dealers and criminal violence all have shocked the world with the brute. The brute symbolizes power in their mind. I never liked their bullying antics and threatening others and I just never liked this kind of thing. The greatest challenge of our hopes and dreams is the good-for-nothing brute. I really do believe this.

Coming from Cayey, high atop mountain in Puerto Rico, almost close enough to touch God did something to me. I was blessed with a warm smile and compassion and respect for others. And I felt close to God. Something was planted in my soul in Cayey and it has thankfully never left me. I just always wanted people to treat one another kindly and treat animals kindly because that was how I was raised and Cayey was that way and in my blood. I just never liked people stealing. I didn't even like someone stealing cookies from a cookie jar.

Even when I was a little kid in the school yard, I didn't like somebody stealing somebody else's lunch. I'd stand there like some sort of grizzly bear when someone would do that stuff. Somehow, I always thought I was put on this earth to protect. And somehow, I always felt it was my responsibility, my duty to do that. Once again, I am getting ahead of myself, but this book is written from my heart and I say it all. Those of you who know me know I don't hold anything back.

I was determined to protect a car, a pearl necklace or a painting that meant a great deal to someone. I was determined to give people a moment of peace, protect the exhibits, stop the kidnappings and calm people down in panic situations. I always wanted to be a cop and strongly enforce laws and protect and serve everyone, equally. It has been my nature and the main ingredient of my soul. I have really learned quite a bit about who I am by writing this book and telling my story.

And so, as life takes me back to a little brown-haired boy running around in a pair of rolled up trousers. I remember drinking coffee with my grandfather. We did that in Puerto Rico and it was the best coffee I have ever tasted. I remember at two being taught to give a good hand-shake. I am a lot older now and those days were a long-time age ago, but I remember them well. Kicking back with my feet on the table, chair tilted back, hands clasped behind my head, I reflect upon my life with a smile and give the world, CAPTAIN BIONIC, *The Amazing Luis Cumba Story of First Responders: America's Everyday Heroes!*

I have written my life story and shot a rocket into literature! Enjoy!

Luis Cumba

PERSONAL NOTE

I spoke to a man a while ago. He was a barricaded suspect in the 1980's. He said he'd been searching for me for almost thirty some years. He met a detective in homicide who knew me. I gave the detective permission to let the gentleman contact me. Initially, the guy calls me and is just talking and talking, asking me if I remember a barricaded gunman situation when he calls me. I tell him I was with the Cleveland Police Department for thirty-two years and have been involved in many barricaded gunmen situations and what's more, I have faced a seemingly endless series of encounters with victims of violent injuries and death. He describes himself and wants to know if I remember him. I can't remember exactly where I saw him and then it starts coming back to me.

I remembered responding to a barricaded suspect situation and we didn't shoot him but instead he was taken to the hospital. I remember visiting him there in the hospital. He goes on to say he tracked me down to tell me that I changed his life. He was grateful that I arrested him. He thanked me for arresting him. When he barricaded himself with the intention of shooting up the neighborhood we talked him out of doing so. We diffused the situation and took him straight to the hospital. I started remembering him well. Thirty some years later, he tracked me down to thank me for arresting him and for visiting him in the hospital. You just can't ask for more than that.

As a career police officer and Lieutenant and Captain, I always made it my utmost priority to protect the innocent. As a first responder and SWAT Commander of Cleveland, I upheld my commitment. **I've put my life on the line many times during my career as a police officer. I've jumped off buildings, crashed cars, broken through windows, hopped over fences, been in explosions and run through fires to rescue someone who needed help. I've put my life on the line for most of my life to help anyone including a cat in a tree. It was my job as a police officer to fight stigmas and fight what gets muted in daily situations because as** a police officer we can only do so much. We are there to enforce the laws. We are put there to try to make the world safe. And every day when I got up in the morning and retired at night I thought hard about the things in life that needed to be changed.

I've broken up brawls, listened to the crazy husband and wife stories and arrested some of the oddest and quirkiest characters on this planet. I've listened to every kind of bedlam you can imagine. I've been a first responder to shootings, kidnappings and when someone was trying to break into a house, I've been there. When someone was being thrown out of a house, I was there, too. It was all part of my job as a police officer to dismiss the danger. I was honored to wear my badge and work with my brothers and sisters in blue and together stand for peace and justice and to always remember we were dealing with human lives. It was our job.

I appreciated the positive aspects of the job and am honored being called a hero. I have been proud to serve and save victims. I am proud to serve with my brothers and sisters in blue. They are mentors, teachers, best friends, sisters and brothers and daughters and sons. In my life I have not experienced an honor greater than serving with first responders. First responders are the highly visible, the ones who rush into the crowd with the mysterious faces that rescue and save but who we somehow never see again. We couldn't survive without them, we couldn't live without them. In disasters and emergencies, they save lives and protect communities. And for the first responders who don't survive in their plight saving others, they leave behind their legacies of strength and heroism.

This book has been written for my brothers and sisters in blue and for all first responders who don't mean to be the heroes they are and who just go to work every single day, rescuing people, putting out fires and trying to save the world. They are America's everyday heroes. God keep them safe.

SOMETHING ELSE

I have contemplated the nature of my heart many times while writing this book and I have come to realize that thinking and feeling are a big part of who I am. But one fine day, after my death, when I was walking downtown in Cleveland, I took the idea seriously to write a book after a friend of mine suggested it. And once I made the decision to write my life story, I resumed my stroll. And then I thought, have I made a terrible decision? I mean, writing a book isn't easy and I don't know how to do it! And then I decided to write my book the Cumba way, right from my heart!

I hope my book will leave those who read it with new perspectives. In these pages you will live my life, visit the places I've visited and experience my journey. Crazy and mystical at times, you will stop at my experiences not as a reader, but as me. You will see me vanish in a string of homicides, bust the shoplifters, tail the druggies, run after the silver and trail the kidnappers. You will also see me land in a coma, die and become Captain Bionic and you will feel my love in every page for God.

I'll always remember the ground
covered in old banana leaves.

I was a little boy under a canopy of trees,
lost in a yellow fruit forest~

Luis Cumba

CHAPTER ONE

Have you ever stumbled across a place that holds such a deep magnetic resonance for you that you remember it all your life? I know the place, Puerto Rico!

I wound along the narrow path, my thin white T-shirt billowing in the wind like a big sail. It pulled me like an aimless wanderer along a path covered in old banana leaves. The sun bowed slightly as I made my way under a canopy of trees that took me deeper and deeper into what became a banana forest. The whole world was full of leaves, blossoms and fruit. Everywhere I looked, there were banana hands waiting to ripen.

Scuffing the dirt in the morning's bloom, I parted the dewed spider webs strung across the way with a twig that was bigger than me. Blending into the classic beauty of what could have easily been a vintage scene on a postcard, I was a little boy in rolled up trousers under the far side of the sky where the banana trees sloped. I had the time of my life as the woody vines hugged me and made me feel part of creation! There is no place like Puerto Rico!

Walking among the red-cupped wild-flowers, I stared at the birds flying overhead. I waved to them thinking how lucky they were to be up so high in the sky! Over and over I'd jump up trying to be with those birds, but I was always too little to reach them. The sun was simple in the blue sky. There were no lanes of cars or traffic lights. No one was widening the roads or digging holes or building a highway. There were no factory fumes, and everything was green, and the ponds and streams were so clear, I could see my face in them. Life was slow moving, light and carefree and everyone knew each other like family.

It has been a long time since the sun sizzled my grandfather's fields in Puerto Rico and I skipped among the dry weeds collecting twigs. It has been a long time since I pretended to be the man, not the little boy, who helped my grandfather tend to the oxen. When I think back about my little boy life, I am dotted with cows and oxen and drawn to the memory of the beauty of the Puerto Rican countryside. It was a place of pure heart. I can still see the oxen's reddish-brown behinds caught in the sunshine! The Puerto Rican sun shined in the afternoon with luster and I was a little boy lost in the orange, banana, lemon and grapefruit trees. But my favorite trees were the plantains that gave shade to the coffee plants. I remember climbing up on the stool in the kitchen and sitting there watching my grandfather grind the beans and make coffee. He had a round mallet hammer and a wooden jar and that's how he crushed the beans, and I watched him, mesmerized.

My grandparents cooked outside. And over the green rolling pastures dotted with horses I ran, not wanting to be late for one of the best Cumba breakfasts of my life! I remember my grandparents well, and I remember running so fast to reach them. They were beautiful people who always greeted me with loads of kisses. Every day was filled with joy and curiosity. Walking along gravelly dirt roads and trying to grab the dangling sunlight, I didn't have to worry about a thing. All I had to do was just grow up under a beautiful blue sky that draped over a green countryside called Cayey (town of the little bull and city of the fog) and I loved it!

Just thinking about my life back then makes me smile. It was paradise! It was just such a wonderful and peaceful place. The most beautiful fragrances filled my nose! Tall rainbowed color flowers that were taller than me filled the air with their beautiful aromas! I cannot put into words how beautiful it all was. The banana forest smelled so fruity and delicious. It was a kind of magical place and I can still feel it to this day. It has been a feeling that has lasted a lifetime for me.

Closing my eyes today, I happily follow those yellow banana blobs hanging from the trees, like it was yesterday. I am a little boy again lost under a yellow sky of banana bunches! It was an enchanted yellow forest that makes me smile as I write this page. That fruit forest was beauty and solitude to this little boy! I have never experienced such a carefree feeling again in my life. And I have just realized that I have not had a decent banana since I left Puerto Rico!

It was a windy dirt road to get up to my grandparent's farm. Not a lot of people had cars back in the day. It was a very high elevation place, Cayey, and the windy dirt road for some reason always made my nose tickle! Maybe it was the clean air that made me always rub my nose! I don't know. But I do know that people were very friendly, very kind and very loving on top of that mountain. Was it the altitude? It was beautiful! And as I think back about my life, I can say that I came from a place where people got along. Again, maybe it was the high elevation of Cayey or maybe it was just what God intended for the people of Puerto Rico, but the serenity has stayed with me a lifetime. Growing up it was place that so peaceful, so serene and so filled with sun. It was a place where you were treated like family even if you were a stranger. A land of hard-earned dollars, framed-family photographs and graciousness, it has always been an honest place of respect.

I still remember running through those fields laughing and being a wild little boy playing in those fields. The faint reddening of a twig in the sun or a mat of dry leaves intrigued me. I was born loving life. Everything got my attention! The trees, the dirt, the hills, the sky, the sun, the rain all seemed to know my name! They all seemed to know about the little boy who so desperately wanted to know about them! I wanted to know about everything! I asked my mother, especially, a lot of questions. She was always there to help me find my footing in the world. Compassionate, she helped me learn a lot about love and kindness and faith. She taught me how to think clearly and with certainty and above all she attended to my feelings. Most of all my mother said my grandfather and I shared the same smile.

Juanita Ortiz Cumba always smelled fresh. Impeccably dressed for any occasion she dressed up for church and always looked nice. My sisters dressed up and us boys always wore a shirt and tie to church. My dad wore a suit and tie and always dressed nice. He bought suits for himself and his sons. My mother was friendly, sociable and was a gifted speaker. When I look back at my mother she was affectionate, warm and gregarious. My mother was very pretty. Everyone remarked how beautiful she was!

Women in church were not permitted to wear make-up back then. The women could only dress up in their dresses. My mother wore different color dresses, and they were always very colorful. My mother was beautiful without make-up. She had beautiful eyes. She was charming and fun. She had a lovely glow about her and everything she said was so memorable. A smile crosses my face when I remember what she would say about flowers. *I don't want any flowers at my funeral. If you want to give me flowers, give them to me when I'm alive!* She was really something, my mother! She knew how to communicate what she felt effectively, and I learned so much from her.

Thinking back about my mother, I remember red was a very nice color on her. She was stunning in red. She wore her beautiful dark hair in a bun high on top of her head! My mother was joy! You couldn't help but feel happy around her. She made everyone feel welcome. My mother lived in unquestioning faith and served and loved her God. She taught us that we can hang out with our friends and that friends have a tremendous impact on us, but that we should hang out with God, too, because God has a big impact on us. I would find out later in my life when I died, the impact that my mother was talking about.

My parents were gems
and they treated their children
like gold~

Luis Cumba

CHAPTER TWO

My mother fussed over me. I was her favorite and everyone in the family knew it. I was her pride and joy, of course we all were, but I really was. My younger brother was a daddy's boy. I loved my dad and mom more than I can ever say. My mom and dad were very different. I really looked up to them both and was honored to work alongside my dad and accompany him on any project he was doing. Funny, I worked alongside of him feeling such joy. He could make anything work. My dad could take rusted junkyard metal and turn it into a car's engine! And my dad had the body language that always told everyone, he could do it!

My father, Julio Cumba had a slow-quick, don't-blink attitude that held steady under anyone's standards. My dad had a strength about him and you didn't tangle with him unless you were prepared for more trouble. On the other hand, he was right there to help you if you were in trouble, especially if you were one of his kids. I think most people were instantly captivated by his tough, charismatic presence or they would visibly retreat from him. As his son, I can only say that working alongside of him made me happy. He had some intangible qualities about him that really resonated with me as a young soul. My dad will always be part of our family's past and future. And just like my mother, he served his God with love.

Dad was quiet and a little bit more on the reserved side compared to my mother's bubbly personality. My dad said a lot without saying anything. It is kind of hard to explain. It was easy to live by the light of his smile and his body language. He had powerful body language. In all my swirls of memory, my dad's body language speaks to me. I remember the time we were all playing ball on the lawn. My dad rarely played ball with us, but out of nowhere he came outside and joined the game. I remember just watching him play. He energized our wills just because of how he was. Sure, he was our dad, but he filled us with expectation and enthusiasm. He had a charm about him. It was his gift.

My mother and father raised God loving children. We would go to church six days a week. We would all get dressed up, all of us! We didn't go to church because we had to go to church. We went to church because we wanted to go to church. My parents taught us to talk about God and tell God everything. They brought God easily into their conversations with us and taught us to understand the need for God in our lives. They let us know to be respectful to God and to each other. They raised us correctly in a very loving environment, each of them loving us in their own special way. I was blessed to have the parents that I did.

My parents were loving parents from the good old days. They gave us a lot of time and a lot of love. They made sure we did things as a family and we in turn loved doing things as a family. We never grudged because we had to do something. That's wasn't the Cumba way. We wanted to be together. We laughed together all the time. Now, of course there were times we may not have gotten along with one another, but it was temporary. All of us grew up with the unconditional love of our parents and we loved them unconditionally, too! We also to this day, love each other, unconditionally. We all grew up with high esteem, with innocence and experience and knowing that if we felt broken to talk to God. He would help fix whatever needed fixing.

I believe that my parent's attitude and philosophies shaped who we were as kids. It was because of my parents that we were confident in ourselves and were filled not only with respect for each other, but for the outside world as well. The Cumba family made great friends and we were always invited to social gatherings because we were fun to be around, and people wanted to be friends with us. We were good folks, great folks and were wonderful to hang around! We loved to laugh and still do. We don't have to be entertained. The simple things in life entertained us. We loved a good joke, a good story about the family and of course my family still loves my singing!

My parents had it down on how to improve our lives and what we could do to improve our lives. They knew love and work. We learned we had to work to make things happen. No one was just going to give us things. We had to earn it and they taught us how. High self-esteem and strong academic performance and confidence were all the keys to building a good and solid life. They had a lot to do with our happiness and our success and always taught us how to be the best version of who we are. They taught us how to love by bringing us up in their love and a loving environment.

One thing that I really learned from my parents was how to use my time efficiently. I have always tried to make the most of my day; grow and thrive! If you just do the minimum of going through the motions with things, you cannot improve as a person. The important thing in life is to understand things the best that you can and ask questions and even though you may not get the answers, keep asking! Some of the major and unexpected lessons I have learned in life came from my parents.

My mother used to tell all of us kids family stories. My mother was a great conversationalist and a great storyteller and a great mother. We were glued to her every word as we learned about our roots and our beautiful heritage. I remember how she would talk about the Cumba family coming from Spain to Puerto Rico in the 1800's. They began as a family of three and they started the Cumba family in Cayey, Puerto Rico. My mother would tell us about our grandpa Pedro who died in World War 1 and that he died so young that it was hard to believe. He fought for this country. She told us all about her father and brothers. Her family was very close. They loved and respected each other. All the brothers and sisters would sit and talk for hours about anything and everything and all the brothers and sisters were the godparents of each other's children. The Cumba family from way back then and now always gives each other a lot of respect. That respect will always exist and the love we have for one another gets stronger every single day. I am proud to be a Cumba!

I will always remember how good my mother and dad were as people and parents. I absorbed their ways just by hanging out with them. My mother loved her children so much and we loved being with her. The boys had to help with the house cleaning because my mother was sick most of her life. We always took care of her. We took her everywhere. We went on a lot of church trips. We went to Canada, Washington DC and Amish country and The White House. My parents loved to travel. My father always wanted to go back to Puerto Rico and that was where he lost his life. My mother was a wonderful person and so was my dad. I loved them very much. They were the best parents ever.

Memories. I love remembering my early life because I lived in a huge place called childhood and it was filled with wonderful things. I think especially important was remembering home. My home was family and good friends. Home was laughter and great food and wonderful evenings and a good spirit. Living in Ohio, making it my home, I always wondered if home was going to mean acquiring a Cleveland accent! Funny the things you remember and the things you think about.

I have a passion for remembering and some of my memories are from the old neighborhood in Cleveland which after a while wouldn't be such a foreign place to me but would be home. But I want to make it clear that I will never forget the gurgling streams or the early morning rooster of Puerto Rico, I not only remember what they looked like, but I can still hear them as if it were yesterday. Sometimes, I wish they were still waking me up! Perhaps, that is what made me a great listener in my life. Early on, I really learned how to use my ears and I kept the gift of great listening throughout my career. I learned so much in school because I really heard what my teachers were teaching. I grew by listening. Maybe it was all due to the early morning rooster jostling me out of bed in its own way and letting me know it was time to get up and start learning about life!

Stories that my mother and grandmother and father and grandfather told me concerning my great-grandparents, great-uncles and aunts really left a lasting impression on me. I wanted to know everything.

Sometimes, I would interrupt with my questions and sit on the edge of my seat to hear their answers. I was a little boy eager for details and everyone who was telling me their stories always knew the answers! Life was beautiful. I loved hearing family stories. When my family told their life stories they were told with such a beautiful storytelling style and spirit and vigor that it has stayed with me my entire life. Isn't that what great storytelling's all about?

Through storytelling you learn about the nature of family, family-centered lessons, traditions, the lure of Christmas, family dinners and more. But most of all, you learn that you can change the world and make it better just like your family before you tried to do. Beneath the varying details of someone's story is a message. Storytelling sets the stage for understanding major life transitions and creates a space for understanding the good stuff and the bad stuff and how to handle the bad stuff. But, more than anything, storytelling, my mother's storytelling, taught me about self-determination and I remember that to this day. There are personal stakes in everything that we do, and I learned this from my mother and my father.

One more thing I learned about my parents were their contributions of kindness and as new generations were born, I learned that kindness has always been special in the Cumba family. My parents invited their children to learn with them and learn we did. I learned so much from them. I learned how they connected fairness to their lives, preserve family traditions as well as handle civic engagements and how to go about to get family approval. The other thing that I learned was that my siblings and I acted independently of one another, each of us carrying our own brand of recognition. I like this because we all are unique.

I believe family pictures were shown along with their stories because they had the knack of connecting the doers to their deeds! My parents loved showing us pictures of who influenced them and who resembles who in the family! Mostly, I think my mother enjoyed storytelling because she loved talking about the family. The stories were inspiring, insightful and she wanted the family to make a tremendous impact on our lives. I loved hearing the family adventures and the best thing about them was they were told with love. My mother and father did everything in the name of love. Their kids were their everything.

All I can say is thank you God, for those beautiful times and for those beautiful memories!

I love you God and I love you Puerto Rico!!!

One time I took a quarter from my mom. She sat me down. She said look Lou if you need something just ask me, don't just take it. After that I never took anything. And I gave my mom back the quarter I stole from her. I felt very badly when I stole that quarter from my mother's bedroom. I could never forgive myself for that. It really upset me so much~

Luis Cumba

The day my mom taught me about stealing
Was the day she stole my heart~

Luis Cumba

CHAPTER THREE

My story illustrates my sensitivity to what I had done. I stole, and I stole from my mother. My mother confronting me about the theft made me feel shame. I must tell you, I felt like absolute crap and my mother's sound advice has sounded in my head for decades. I feel especially fortunate that my mother called me out the way she did at such an early age. It made a huge difference in my life later. My mother was sincere, and I owe her a debt of gratitude. Her encouragement and advice always seemed poetic, and I remember her this way. It wasn't her style to ask me all sorts of questions about what I was doing. What she did was make sure that I was okay. She never asked me where I was all the time because she knew I was handling myself appropriately. None of my siblings every got in any trouble. I never got in any trouble either. But, I do remember a moment when my life changed and so here is the story.

I remember one day I wanted to buy something at the store, but I didn't have any money. My mom had a quarter in her bedroom and I took it. And when she found out I stole it, she sat me down and told me I should never do that. She said it was stealing and stealing was wrong. If you want something, ask me for it. I still remember the way she told me that. She was gentle. She was so compassionate. I think I hurt her that I did that. She felt bad that I stole it from her and I felt terrible that I did it. I was just five years old at the time and I gave her back the quarter. Years later, she lent me money for my first car and I paid her back and I gave her the first ride in it.

I really felt so awful about stealing that quarter from my mom though. It shook me up that I did that. The situation really touched me. What could I do but just store what I did in my heart? I did it and that was all there was to it. I didn't have much choice as to how to handle it after the fact of it. My mom let it go, but I just couldn't seem to let it go. I knew that I had to make my mom proud of me. I think that stealing that quarter from my mom made me want to be a policeman. I believe it was my first inkling that I wanted to be in law enforcement. She really instilled in me how bad it was to steal and I wanted to be on the right side of the law and do good things and protect people from those who do bad things and steal. She taught me right from wrong and the life lesson stuck.

Stealing can lead to being arrested. I didn't want that. And I knew I didn't want to disappoint my mother anymore than I had. I don't think she ever told my dad what I did either. She just carried the hurt herself of what I did. So, I knew I had to look within myself and find peace, but how? How could I make my mom totally believe in me again and then I figured out how to make this happen. I had to be worthy of her respect and find value in myself. And so, I learned from the best teachers in the world, my parents!

I learned from both my parents how to be a quality person and never take advantage of anyone, especially them. You want something, you work for it or you ask for it. That was my parent's motto and that became my motto. I was my dad's number one helper. My dad and I built the basement in our house. I learned how to cut wood and hammer a nail because of my dad. We really related, and I helped him all the time. He taught me how to do carpentry, plumbing and how to do electrical work. He showed me how to wire things. He taught me how to fix cars. My dad was a quiet guy. He didn't say much. We worked side by side together, but we never had a real conversation. He taught me all these different professions so that I would never go hungry. My parents wanted me to be able to take care of myself. My dad taught me so much in his own special way and mom was always there to show me the love.

Funny, you never looked my dad in the eye. Hispanics are taught you don't look at authority in the eye. This is the trait of my beautiful Puerto Rico. In the Hispanic culture it is disrespectful to do this, but in the white culture they think you are lying if you don't look someone in the eye. This was quite a culture shock for me here in the US mainland.

It was hard to grasp the opposing ideologies. I had to observe things differently and interact in different ways, but I acclimated. I had to acclimate to effectively deal with society. It was important for me to fit in and live in this new culture.

My parents both had very high standards and they instilled them in their children. They were both very different from each other, but they were both strong and were honest on what they believed in and who they were as people. My dad was physically strong and had the biggest hands that I've ever seen to this day. His hands were huge! He had huge fingers! He had a classical guitar made for his fingers because they were so big! My dad protected us, but believe me, you didn't want to get hit by those hands! Those hands appeared to be just about indestructible, let me tell you!

My parents were very nice-looking people. They had that beautiful Puerto Rican look about them. Something I just can't explain. But there is a certain vivaciousness that Puerto Ricans have about them. They look exotic but down-to-earth. There is so much warmth in the culture. There is a warmth about the Island and the people. My mother and dad had this warmth. They were amazing people and I never wanted to disappoint them. They were both so smart about everything. There were so many interesting things about them that I will treasure the rest of my life, especially their wisdom and their warmth.

I loved the fun and carefreeness that composed the Puerto Rican air! I just loved it! It made you feel so alive! Running through the Puerto Rican heat, my little shorts slung low above my knees. I was a little boy who pretended he was a man in charge of the cows and the oxen! I tossed my little boy hair out of my eyes, my bare feet taking me in the direction of the heavenly aroma of frying eggs and my grandfather making breakfast! Could he cook! Over the green rolling pastures dotted with horses I ran, not wanting to be late for one of the best Cumba breakfasts of my life! I remember my grandfather well and I remember running so fast that my thin little t-shirt billowed in the wind and made me look like a sail when I reached him!

Now, everything is hot about Puerto Rico! The country is beautiful, the landscape is gorgeous, the food is to die for and I already told you the women and the lemon and orange trees are more than interesting talk. But there is something about being beneath the Puerto Rican sun that pushes away the snide comments of the day and allows you to let go of all that bothers you. It is called karma! Puerto Rico has great karma! It just has a wholeness about it and I think it was instilled in my gene pool! I have felt this Puerto Rican karma since I was old enough to remember things. Maybe this karma came from the spine of the mountains and the flow of the rain. Maybe it comes from the stillness of a stolen moment when everything goes quiet and you are filled with that Puerto Rican feeling of peace.

Puerto Rico has charisma and an enchantment that has remained with me that few may understand. Puerto gave me vitality and remains an unforgettable portrait in my mind. It made me somebody at a very early age. I remember at three years old my grandfather gave me a stick and asked me to help him tend to the oxen. I lightly swished at them on the back to get them to move. I tapped them lightly. To this day, I still hope I didn't hurt them. You see that is karma. Being a good person, a decent person is good karma. Nice goes around let me tell you. I learned that in Puerto Rico and it stayed with me. That is good karma and good karma is having compassion for all that you touch and for all that touches you. That is Puerto Rican karma and that is the peace that enriches lives and that is the karma that is in my hometown!

I think the great appreciation that I have for life and God comes from my parents love and from sitting beneath the Puerto Rican sun! It was so magnifying, so enriching and so spiritual. Go to Puerto Rico and you will know your heart. I can't explain it. But I know my heart. Yes! I know my heart. But I know my heart even more since I died which reveals one of the reasons that I have written this book. It is important to listen to your heart, reveal your flaws and be aware of your good qualities. Through my childhood, I began to understand how the world was educating me and I began to understand the importance of learning. After I died and came back to life, I would remember everything I ever learned.

But the thing that I really learned was love and appreciation and respect for ownership and it is in this way I began to imagine my future. My mother taught me the day I stole from her that respect for someone must be unthinking and automatic. Interesting, it is not hard to steal. If you want to steal art, you can just take it off the wall. Paintings can be cut out of frames and be whisked away. Small items can be tucked into bags and carried off and jewelry can easily be secreted away never to be spotted again by its owner. Now, of course, there are exceptions when you have a cop or a security guard or someone with authority waiting in the wings and you get caught but true criminals base their thoughts on the art of stealing and monetary reward.

My mother made me realize a lot in my life about stealing. She made me realize that theft delineates a type of character and I wasn't that person. Ripping off and robbing under any situation is wrong. I learned the nature of ownership and the justifications for ownership. I realized that you must protect someone's feelings and that stealing someone's belongings is hurtful and harmful. My mother taught me that stealing is worthless and although I stole from my mother that day, I never stole her beauty. She handled that situation with beauty and class and I learned that day that I would never be thrown to the side of crime and from that point on I started dreaming about being a cop. I had predictable energy and it was filling me up everyday with the feeling of law enforcement.

Although it has been a very long time since I wore my grammar school graduation robe, I still remember how badly I wanted to learn how to protect and serve. I thought about it all the time. I wanted to serve the public, but I was just a little kid. I was stuck. Even at eleven years old I was willing to show off my impressive skills and hard work to show everyone what I was made of, but I couldn't figure out what to get involved in that would relate to me being a cop and then it came to me! I became captain of the school's safety patrol and I really liked it and I was praised by the teachers who told me I did a great job! I liked making my classmates feel safe and the younger children feel protected. I wouldn't allow kids to intimidate other kids. I didn't like that. And I would step in if I saw something happening and stop any bullying even if I didn't know the kids involved. There were no fights and no name-calling on my watch and the kids knew it and they didn't even try. I kind of took after my dad in that way. I had acquired his presence and you know what? I just now realized this as I am journaling my thoughts!

You didn't cross my dad. Like I have mentioned, my dad had the biggest hands I have ever seen, and you didn't want to get hit by those hands! Well, although I don't have the hands my dad had, I have his presence. There has always been a toughness about me that no one wants to tangle with even to this day, if they know what is good for them. Isn't that funny how it just hit me while writing this paragraph how much I have grown to be like my dad! The ironies of like are cooking up the truth of my story as I write this book. When I was helping dad work, it was not an ordinary assignment. It was my chance to be like him!

I brought good-humored toughness to situations even as a little kid and so I loved this job and I realized that my job as captain of the school's safety patrol would be something that I would remember the rest of my life. It allowed me to be provided with the current events of the school day and it also gave me a few doses of inspiration while I was getting involved in it all. When I think back about it I realize now how it confirmed my longing to be a cop and that alone makes me grin to this day!

We never could complain about
What our parents didn't give us
Because they gave us
Everything they had~

Luis Cumba

CHAPTER FOUR

I remember I helped my dad plant the grass at church. I liked working side by side with my dad on projects. We didn't talk much. We just planted the grass, but it felt good working with my dad. There was something about him when he worked. It is something that I have never forgotten not just because it moved me deeply, but because it was so honestly him. He loved working. Seeing him work was really a candid look into his life. He had an unshakable faith in God, in himself, in his family and in his birthplace, Puerto Rico.

America was big in my dad's heart and it rubbed off on all his kids. His approach to life was work hard and have strong ethics and morals, believe in God and do things that you can be proud of and thing that will make your family proud. I absorbed his attitude to life and it made me strong and independent. But, it also was instilled in me that as a family we could do things together and have fun!

We were a nice normal family from Puerto Rico. We were a family of laughter who didn't give up even when things got hard. A family of storytellers, we didn't know the meaning of boring. I personally was never bored, and we didn't even have a tv set when we were growing up! So, we learned to listen to family stories and make our own fun, but we never got into any trouble. We were filled with stories that keep families together and I loved listening to them. We had so many incredible moments as a family. I loved listening to them all and I especially loved the family sense of humor and the warmth that made us all sleep so good at night. Growing up in my family made me experience the lovable side of life.

It reminds me of the time that my family and I took a visit to see my aunt and uncle in Philly and their kids. My father was very close to his brothers and sisters. We loved to visit them. We stayed with

Aunt Monin's family and their kids and we all got along and ate and laughed together. One trip really sticks out to me and that was the time I went with my cousins to see the movie, *The Ten Commandments.* I will never forget the cinematic experience! It ranks to this day as one of the most euphoric experiences in my life! It was pure cinematic inspiration. Built with staggering brilliance, the movie theater was a swirling masterpiece! It was an iconic classic experience. The movie screen was so big. I couldn't take my eyes off the big screen and the theater was so huge! I felt like I was in the cosmos.

A classic performance in every shot, *The Ten Commandments* remains my favorite movie of all time! What an experience! I am sitting here and smiling when I think about the glinting lights before they dimmed and how I got my popcorn and sank into the deep soft theater seats. The dark cool movie theater and the big movie screen was so exciting! It was a great place to stay cool and the seats were so soft. I imagine myself there right now. Never had I experienced something like this before. I was sitting there in that movie theater with my heart pounding like crazy, waiting for the movie to start! And then in an explosion of quiet, the movie theater went dark and I became glued to the movie. My arms were resting on top of the arm rests, and I remember I did not move an inch on my soft sunken seat for fear that I may miss one word of the movie.

After the movie I just stayed in my seat until the last credit left the screen. And I knew that I loved Hollywood! I loved going to the movies and from that moment on, the movie theater had a place for me in the city's sprawl. It was part of the landscape! The movie theater became a landmark to me like a train station and an airport! Everywhere I went, and every time I passed by a movie theater it was like those move theaters rose up to greet me! Those movie theaters somehow seemed to know how much I loved them! I loved the movies and their sense of place! It made me feel so alive!

I remember that day when we finally left the movie theater, we left with smiling faces. I couldn't believe the experience and I thought about it for a very long time! I was so happy and so impressed with the movie I couldn't sleep that night. I was wide awake. I couldn't stop thinking about the experience. I was on my bed for hours thinking about the dark movie theater and the padded seats and the big screen and the movie, *The Ten Commandments!* And although that movie was part of a bygone era, it remains my favorite movie of all time. It was delivered in such a powerful way that I couldn't take my eyes off the screen. The colors, and clothes and acting and the delivery of it all mesmerized me as well as the special effects. I had never seen anything like this before. Charlton Heston was absolute celebrity and the story was not only a memorable performance but was so eventful! It packed quite a punch! I suppose that every era gets the beautiful recognition that it deserves. But, for whatever it is worth, that experience spoke brilliantly to a Puerto Rican kid in Philly and made him feel so alive! Rest in Piece uncle Juan, cousin Willy and John.

I absolutely loved those visits to Aunt Monin in Philly! We all loved those visits and my parents helped me understand the meaning of family and morals and ethics and life if that makes sense. I learned as much as I could about everything. I learned that stability and spontaneity were both important in life and family is everything! Religion was important as was God, but also loving one another and having fun was important, too. My parents instilled in me that it was okay to take time to think. And I have practiced that every day of my life.

My parents did their best in life. I can't say it any better except just like that. Both were deacons in the church. They were bright even though they had little education. Life worked its will with them. Maybe it was their sense of wonder that made them so wonderful or maybe it was their sense of family. I don't know. But they were filled with the kind of love and obligation to life that you pray for in people. They had it, that love and obligation. Boy, did they have it and it showed in their every step. And then there was the unthinkable tragedy that turned my family upside down. My father got shot and killed in Puerto Rico. To this day, we are all so sad about the way my dad died. I am very sentimental and shaken about it after all these years. I still remember at the trial how I jumped over the seat and went after the guy who killed my dad. The police had to restrain me.

My parents didn't make any excuses. They told it like it was and expected their eight children to do the same. The Cumba family was composed of four boys and four girls. Carmen, Luis Alberto (me!), Martin (a great speaker) and Margie, Rosie, Julio and Pedro and there was Irma, the baby. We were a functioning family. We all got along with each other and we loved being with one another. It was really something! We loved spending time as a family together. The family was firmly planted in love and we blossomed every day in decency, intelligence and couth. We honored our parents and they honored us. And we all not only loved each other, we liked each other and were great friends growing up and still are today!

At first glance anyone who knew The Cumba's knew we were good folks. We enjoyed good clean fun. We never got into any trouble and as a family we managed to get by during difficult times without getting involved in crime or dealings that were against the law. We never did anything against the law. None of my brothers and sisters or me ever got into any drugs or drinking. We were never a problem and we never got into fights or trouble. We were great kids who loved to play stick ball and play as a family. I remember one day that my father came out and played stickball with us. It was a big occasion because he didn't usually do that. He was busy working all the time. I remember watching him play and to this day it is a beautiful memory of mine.

My father was surely very important to me and to all of us. He was inspiring and had a personal feeling for humankind. My father had winning ways. He instilled in us fairness and to treat all people with respect. I don't even remember who won that game. We were all winners in that game because my dad played with us! I have the most enduring beautiful memories of my mother's soft ways and my dad's protectiveness and how they used to talk to us (their children).

My family was and still is a source of comfort and support for me.

Old values were instilled in us growing up and they made us resilient. More than anything, each of my brothers and sisters and myself have become followers of our parents, but at the same time we emerged with our own likes and dislikes and our own gifts. We established common bonds with one another but also acknowledge our differences. We have always given one another tireless support. We valued our shared interests. Once again, looking back, I can say, I had the best parents a kid could have, and I was blessed with the best family a kid could have.

The Cumba family has always had their own beautiful love for God and it shows in our respect for people we meet and the friends that we have. Friends have always been very important. The Cumba family and all my brothers and sisters and my parents have always been a very welcoming group. This comes from our Puerto Rican heritage. People could feel it in our presence. There is a certain warmth that we have, and it will always be with us. We grew up in warmth and grew up in a very loving environment. Our home was a welcoming one and everyone always felt so comfortable around the Cumba family. We just seemed to spark a special bond with all who we met.

We made warm-hearted friends and were very loyal to our friendships. After growing up together we have remained incredibly close as brothers and sisters and we remain close to our friends who are always part of our family. And, I think it is because of my loving home environment that I have such a high regard for friendship. Friends are very dear in Puerto Rico. Friends come with lots of food and big fun gatherings and lots of laughter! My family has always loved to show their love to friends with warm greetings and lots of laughter!

I believe my beautiful family has brought light to me about the way I see the world. My reflective comments about growing up come to me so easily because of them and the loving childhood I had. Writing about growing up is so vivid in my mind as well as the outlandish stuff I used to do! There have been some crazy times that sticks to my memory. And ever since I can remember my strength has been in generating excitement! No one has ever been bored in my company! Really, I can't imagine sitting down for one second and thinking that I'm bored or that I'm boring. I've always had the passion for self-invention!

I don't just glimpse the road to happiness
I travel it~

Luis Cumba

CHAPTER FIVE

Every situation that I have ever experienced has given rise to genuine feelings. I believe this is the reason life has always been fun and exciting. I have always lived my life in high spirits, yet I have been my critic-at-large. I've been blessed with the ability to come up with new ideas and that is a must in life. You've always got to try new things, so life doesn't become stale. When people do the same thing all the time then you get into a routine where you don't try new things. Originality must be alive and well in life! I've never had a problem coming up with new ideas.

I've never been afraid to leave my comfort zone. Now don't get me wrong living a smooth life make people comfortable, but I never liked to fall into the trap of never changing and never improving. Ever since I was a little boy I was highly ambitious to push myself and be an opportunist. Who would know that in years to come my *big break* story would come in law enforcement and I would soar to the top! Think of things that are never possible and do them! You've got to be energized by life! Every day is a day of opportunity. I can honestly say that I have lived every day to the fullest and have ever since I was a kid.

I have had an array of interests over my life, but the academic world really seemed to grab me early on in my life. Political Science was an important part of my personal development at college. It seemed to foster my interests and inspired my personal development as a historian and civil rights expert. I think majoring in political science really enhanced what I am all about. I was very attracted to it. The study of politics and power not only in the United States but internationally really caught my eye. I loved learning political ideas, understanding policies, ideologies and behavior as well as diplomacy, strategy, law and the components that drive nations to war. My studies in political science really helped me to become an expert on the Holocaust along with my great professor. Government studies has always held an inter-est for me. It was interesting that all types of power relationships exist in human interaction. I began to understand power relationships and the various fundamental problems facing society. Studying political science helped me to understand the problems of maintaining world peace and understanding life through friendships and rivalries.

Studying the world was a new terrain of study for me. I learned about how to reconstruct the world so that people could get along and nations could get along better. Troubled by conflict from an early age, I excelled in my college courses in political science and my vision for the future. Strongly influenced by a distaste for established disciplines I realized that road building has had a strong impact on my life. Road building friendships, good relationships along with road building a successful career was all very important to me. It became my discipline.

I was glad I had bought the Old's. I happily passed all the other cars on the road. Its energies awakened mine in a way that to this day I still cannot describe. It just downright delighted me. I drove along in an experience that I had never had before. I liked the privacy and solitude it gave me. That Old's was my trailblazer. That car rocked!

Luis Cumba

It was a gold Oldsmobile
And it looked like a Cadillac
And when I drove it I felt like a million bucks

Luis Cumba

CHAPTER SIX

It was an Old's and it looked like a Cadillac and it rocked! Sleek with an image like no other car on the road that Old's was filled with world class refinement and, no doubt was certified badass! Remembering it now I get a huge grin across my face. It was one heck of a car! It was a 1972 Old's Classic, and it was flashy gold— a gold flashy car and it was beautiful. It rocked! It was built very similar to a Caddy and it made me feel like a million bucks and then some when I drove it. It was the granddaddy of the classy cars! And I took care of it like it was gold, always washing and waxing it. A work of art, I hit the streets with it like a golden lamp in a green night!

Behind the wheel of this flashy want-to-be Caddy, I was the sexiest man alive! I was convinced all the girls were looking at me, wanting a date and I was convinced this car would bring me name, fame, glory and fortune! It was an upmarket car and better than anything around! Eat your heart out Jaguars, I would think as I cruised along in the glamour vehicle! But alas, like all of Hollywood's vast magic tricks my time was short-lasted feeling like a movie star behind the wheel t as I got pulled over by a cop! It was the beginning of a dark time for me and my realizations. Let me explain.

I was Luis Cumba a Hispanic in Long Island in the 1970s and it wasn't the easiest of times. It wasn't all shiny and Hollywood for me. It was a bizarre start for a Hispanic like me. The world was filled with a jumble of bigotry and me, Luis Cumba in Long Island and a teen in the 1970s was in the thick of it. So, I dressed nice and found my niche in feeling good, living wittily and enjoying life. I was a naturally radiant type of guy. I was dark-haired, dark-eyed and almost hand-some! Wait! I wasn't almost handsome, I was downright handsome! I was one handsome Hispanic and from an early age, I was sweeping women off their feet and I didn't know it and now I had the gold Olds! However, it didn't change my situation. It seemed like the cops had it in for minorities. And, there was no way out of the system if you were Hispanic and it was a crying shame.

It seemed as if the cops in Long Island only saw the brown shadow upon my face or maybe they were all bored cops who had this great time with cruising around with the sirens, the lights and all that sort of stuff and going after minorities. I don't know. I was startled and surprised and horrified all at the same time. What in heck was wrong with them? Still to this day when I think about it, I am filled with a shudder of horror and disappointment. I was a good person. My family were good people. We were great people! I will talk more about this later in future chapters, but for now, I was just a guy from Puerto Rico! It was strange because in one minute the real state of situations flashed like lightning across my bewildered brain and in the next second, I thought this can't really be happening. Once I started to realize racism, I couldn't take it. I mean was this modern policing? It couldn't be. I couldn't stand it. I couldn't stand police misconduct which included, false arrest and intimidation of any kind. It really bothered me, and I couldn't stand that, and I was a product of it all because of the color of my skin.

I remember it was in my late teens and I started taking tests to be a policeman. I also remember I was stopped a few times by the cops for no good reason and that truly bothered me. I was being picked on, but why? What did I do? And then it hit me. There were not many Hispanics living on Long Island and I remember being stopped driving to church one day. I was driving someone else's car and I completely forgot about the ticket that was attached to that car because it wasn't my car and I got stopped for that and razzed. There was no reason for that. I was a fun guy and I enjoyed life and I wasn't going to get slowed down by bigotry.

So, I had the gold Olds. The car played a hilarious role in my life. Remembering it now at length, I get this huge smile across my face when I think about it! It was one hell of a car! And so like I said, it was a 1972 Olds Classic and it was flashy gold— a gold flashy car and it was beautiful. I felt like I was part of the modern celebratory collection of vehicles with that Old's! An emblematic figure of a car its large wheels and massive whoosh of power got me wherever I went in style. Everywhere I drove, I drove in sleek gold and boy, could it go fast! I believe to this day that vehicle was jet-inspired and so was I! Now that I think about it, that Olds was like the Batmobile! It had that cyclone-concept attached to it and I felt like a real superhero when driving it. That Olds was undeniably radical! It was just one heck of a cool car and I loved it! It was iconic.

It was my preferred mode of transportation and it had Hollywood appeal to it! It had Cadillac flavor to it. It was jaw-dropping and turned the heads of everyone on the road because the car was classy. It had car charisma and voyeurism and beauty to it! It could have been picked for a Hollywood movie, that car! And it was a creator of performance. Boy could that car handle the road! It was an Olds filled with Cadillac moments! Yes! I loved that car! It was a fantastically one-of-a-kind automobile.

I was hard working and making good money for a teen in the early 1970s. Everyone who knew me was aware of my work ethics. I was working in this mental institution in Brentwood Long Island. I got the job right after high school. Instead of going straight to college, I worked with the mental patients on the night shift. I was a care-giver. We had patients that were institutional patients and I took care of them. They were bipolar patients—one minute they loved me and next minute they hated me. That was my night job and I did my best to give the patients compassion and understanding and respect. I believe in respect.

I got a day job as a mechanic. It was the opposite of my night job. This job was operational. I became the classic American success story filled with life lessons and soon I had enough money to help my family and support myself. I was successfully engaged in business. I fixed cars all day and I learned from the best! My father taught me how to fix cars. So, I was a natural at it and I did quality work. Fixing cars had a positive influence on my state of mind. I was proof that prosperity awaited hard workers.

I never saw life in obstacles. Of course, there were challenges but there was no such a thing as obstacles. There were challenges in life and although you couldn't always deal with them as a superhero, the Cumba way was you meet your challenges head on. I'm not going to say that I made it every time, but I sure as heck tried to be an achiever in life. I didn't allow my challenges to cast a dark shadow on my life. Somehow, I just kept plugging forward. I wasn't gold-fevered, but I wanted my family to be comfortable and I wanted the chance at success. I wanted to experience the magical feeling of making it and the exciting feeling of earning money and helping my family. It was my driving force in life and the Olds was the vehicle to do it! I liked the way it made me feel. And while my Olds didn't have the type of gadgets that made the Batmobile so cool, it had what it took to make me feel awesome!

I never forgot how I learned from my dad. I loved learning from him. I loved working side by side with my dad, but I also learned to fix cars out of necessity! I had to make the car run so I could use it to go somewhere otherwise I would be stuck at home and I needed to see the world! It makes me smile to this day how I fixed the car, so I could get out of the house. My dad felt that this was one way to keep me at home—if cars, at home didn't work!

Now, I didn't want my dad on my tail, but I was young and wasn't about to stay at home all the time. My world was jumping with places and things to do! The nights were filled with eye-catching color! There was the fast-food scene and patty melts and lumps of ice cream and I wanted to hang out and check it out! And so, I had to fix the car! So, sliding around on the grease puddles in the garage was worth it because I became one heck of a mechanic!

I remember it like it was yesterday. My dad would take apart the ignition of the car, so I wouldn't be able to use the car, so I wouldn't go anywhere! So, I learned how to fix stuff and that is how I got the car running! I loved my dad, but I was a kid! I was ready to see and experience life! I loved working with my dad, but we hardly ever exchanged a word. So, I had the flashy gold car that I mentioned, and it was a big car. There were not very many Hispanics on Long Island back in the day, so I was stopped quite a bit by the cops because of my nationality and I didn't think it was right. We were good people. We were good kids. All of us kids went to church on Sundays. We didn't play craps or anything. The situation influenced me because I thought people should be treated better than that and that was the start of me wanting to be the cop that treated people right and-in-the-future when I became a cop, I did just that!

It is interesting now that I think about it, my idea to really pursue being a cop was due to so many things, but one thing that stands out is prejudice. There was something mysterious about being a crime-fighter that I found to be very alluring. There was something superhero about it and something viscerally American in the way the superhero forks out justice. Nothing is out of the question in life. I learned that from my parents. Everything in life is worthy of investigation and exploration. You never know what is going to award you recognition in some way. You never know what in life is going to make you feel that you have reached your true potential.

I have always felt that we are all here for some reason. We are here to contribute something to society. I really do believe that. Remember, everyone has a calling and I can pull up no other memory that my parents when I say this. My parents instilled in all of my siblings that we are all unique and have our own heroism about us. We all have our own contributions to society. Whether we are part of the academic and scholarly community or part of an industry's workforce there are no limits what you can do.

And as far as that gold Olds goes, it was one badass car that cheered me on in life! It had so much Hollywood flair to it, it should have been in the movies!

I chuckle when I think about my dad
Breaking the car so I wouldn't be able to go out at night.
And to think, I grew up to be a cop and work some of the
Meanest streets of not only Cleveland but the
United States~

Luis Cumba

CHAPTER SEVEN

I brought to law enforcement a generous dimension and a sympathetic spirit, but everyone knew I was tough. I was tough and fair. I never abandoned situations as hopeless. I was a cop of strong character and I maintained a balanced mind regarding every situation that confronted me as a policeman. I adjusted my temperament. When I was involved in a case, it absorbed all my attention. Buried among my books my fierce nature of studying deeply attracted me to the study of crime. I have always had extraordinary powers of observation in following clues and clearing up mysteries which somehow may have been abandoned by someone who felt a case was hopeless. I always held out for a better choice if I could.

My manner and attitude in law enforcement was also my attitude in my personal life. I easily tackled new problems and issues. I had a kindly-eye and would walk through the community. I wasn't clumsy or careless on the job. I responded immediately when needed. I listened to someone give their reasons in the department before I made any kind of judgement. I made strong friendships within the department and was excellent at making distinctions and understanding and analyzing material I was presented with. I was never one-sided in evaluating any situation. I never imagined what something meant, I analyzed the evidence and was very thorough.

I never took on the liberty of doubting. I had to be certain. I piled fact upon fact and I never glanced the facts, I read everything in detail. I studied fact upon fact until I was comfortable with my conclusions. The strangest and most out of the ordinary situations had to be evaluated properly. I never jumped to conclusions. I never got caught up in the grips of impatience. I took my time and took my time to give attention to detail t in every crime. I learned early on to greet impatience and anger with composure. In turn I greeted questions with information, facts and answers and stood my ground on what was right even if it appeared wrong at the time. And I always tried to understand frustration and grief and I understood early on that compassion is important. I was there to protect, serve and help as a cop. Being rude never solves a problem. I also learned early on as a cop on the street that each situation is unique and being patient and understanding stops a crowd from getting angrier and utmost in my mind is that I was there to help, serve and keep the peace. I had the presence and still do of the tough guy and that I didn't take any bull, but I was also there to be fair.

Police officers are public servants. A career of fighting crime must be felt from the heart. Patrolling the streets is a big deal. Academy training was tough and always will be. The physical fitness was absolutely, grueling, but I did it and am better for it. There were times when I really enjoyed it. The training is difficult toady just like it was back in my dad. I did very well. I was proud that I succeeded academically and physically. Ever since I was a little kid I had what it takes to be a police officer.

And I want to say that being a police officer is not just a job. It is a career and it is a life. You must gear yourself to respond to all sorts of calls, some of which may be tragic. Abuse, injuries, accidents death and abuse become part of your everyday life.

Dealing with victims of crime and families of lost loved ones is very hard. Your life changes. It seems as if every moment you are someone else as you deal with something else. You don't call it a day at 5pm. It really is like you are married to your job and you don't know if you are going to make it back home at the end of the day. Anything can happen in the day of a police officer. And as I think back about my life, I am taken back to the instance about how my dad used to take apart the car in some way, so I couldn't go anywhere, and I had to assemble so I could go out. He was worried about me going out on the town! Who in the world would know, I would grow up to patrol some of the meanest streets of America! Funny how things work out!

It is not about walking down the Ivy League hallways of a University and boasting about where you went to college. It is not about just hanging out in school because you don't want to work. What it is about is stuffing a duffle bag of clothes, embarking off into the world with well-earned impressive credentials and a heart full of drive and determination and make the world better~

Luis Cumba

CHAPTER EIGHT

I graduated from Cleveland State University in downtown Cleveland, Ohio. I majored in Political Science and minored in Law and Labor Relations. I am a scholar of American presidents and studied the Holocaust. As a matter of fact, my Jewish professor was a concentration camp survivor from the death camp, Auschwitz. She was a great speaker. She integrated social learning with emotional learning, providing experiences that created memories for me as if I were in Auschwitz even though I wasn't there to experience the brutal situations first hand. Her teaching was constructive, real and impressive and I became immersed in the content, studying the Holocaust with fervor! I absorbed so much content in such a passionate way that today, I am considered by many an expert. My Holocaust Professor was so impressed with me and my ability to absorb the material we keep in touch and she sends me a holiday card every year.

I remember I wanted to know everything about the Nazi camps and the Holocaust. I read so intensely and so passionately that I couldn't break away from the material. I thought about the brutal concentration camps, the experiments and the suffering and it really bothered me. I couldn't tear myself away from the content. I read about the starving children who wore the striped pajama concentration camp attire.I read about the little children who faced the Nazi machine guns. I was absolutely tortured by the brutality and the starvation. I was a non-Jew, a Puerto Rican American completing identifying with the Jews who were slaughtered at the hands of racism and hate at its worst.

Every single story that I read impacted me in ways that I find very difficult to explain. Where was the humanity of the world? Clearly, the Jews could not believe their fate and perhaps this is the reason that they stayed in the country and didn't leave when they have could have. They couldn't believe something like this could happen to them or any race and religion of people. As a non-Jew I couldn't believe it either and my instructor could see the passion I had as a student. She remarked time and time again how impressed she was with my concentration on everything that I was reading but also with my emotions. I couldn't accept what had happened. It brought me back to when I was a youngster and didn't like kids being mistreated and I always tried to protect the kids in my class who were not being treated properly.

I found the study of the Holocaust to be so moving and man's inhumanity so devastating that I would get emotional about it. The persecution was horrendous. From the moment I started reading about the Holocaust I could hear the sobs and shouts of the Jews. The more I read, the more I learned the more I felt an obligation to continue reading and studying and discussing everything. So many innocent lives taken away. I started thinking about the contributions those people who were exterminated could have made, the lives they may have made better and how the world may have missed out on people who could have cured cancer or made great discoveries.

I couldn't ignore what I was reading, and I couldn't understand how the world ignored for so long what was happening. In the end six million Jews were slaughtered. The Jewish genocide clearly conveys that there is evil in the world and similar killings have happened with other cultures. The reality of the German terror in the world at this time rings loudly in my life and as I say, I am a non-Jew, but I felt it, I felt the suffering. One doesn't have to be a particular group that is suffering to feel the suffering. We are all human beings. We can all relate to suffering and injustice. I identified so strongly with those Jews in the concentration camps that it kept me up at night.

As an expert on the Holocaust I was incredibly interested in getting my hands on as much material as I could. Hitler was a paranoid leader and the Jews not realizing that anything like this could ever happen to them were too passive. In years to come, as a police officer I would find that I didn't like to use force but if I needed to neutralize a situation I would use any means I could, but it wasn't my first choice. I think it is very important to assess a situation properly. If the Jews had done that from the beginning perhaps more could have gotten to safety. But, one must keep in mind that the world was and still in chaotic.

Now, I have always been a man who reaches for answers. This is one of the reasons I was such a great cop. As an expert on the Holocaust I still cannot understand the silence of the world in the face of the slaughter of the Jews in WW2. I still struggle to find meaning in the complex stories of whose who remained bystanders during the Holocaust when people were being gassed. Bystander stories have different perspectives that raise different questions, but I still cannot help but ask how could the world have witnessed these monstrous crimes and continued like nothing was happening for so long?

I have always been troubled by the bystander. As a cop, I could not be a bystander to anything, but I never was a bystander to anything before I was a cop. It wasn't who I was as a person and is not who I am today. The subject is complicated. I realize it is impossible to stand up and respond to every crisis or even personal encounter. The study of the Holocaust has taught me many things, but the one thing that really sticks out to me is it shows how important it is for people to develop an understanding of the Holocaust and all things that are racist and tragic. It is important to become moved as a person to contribute compassion and understanding and ideas on how to create a more humane world. People must get involved to stop suffering and oppression.

As a Holocaust Expert, I related to the Holocaust and to human suffering and oppression. As such, I think it is wise to pay attention to people who hate and decry injustice wherever it may be. In life it is very difficult to lose what is dear. I must ask a question to the world, as long as there is hate how can there ever be peace on earth? As a police officer I wanted to bring peace to all walks of life, peace and safety. Unconditional love is a must and not turning our backs on horror and inequality is a must too. There must be justice for all.

I must go back to my time at Cleveland State and the humanities class which inspired me to research civil rights and abuses in this country and ultimately become a Civil Rights Expert. The class took a long look at one of the darkest times the world has ever known. The course first began with Ivan The Terrible in Russia and his long reign of terror. Regarded as one of the cruelest men in history he is one of the best-known Russian Tsars. Neglected and hungry as a child, he grew up with a hatred for the nobility and sacked Russia in bloodshed and brutality in the history books. I couldn't believe what I read about Ivan the Terrible in Russia and it made me want to research a lot more on my own. Unfortunately, Ivan the Terrible is hardly the last of the horrors.

The savagery of the Holocaust goes well beyond this chapter in its atrocities and evil doings. The terrors and sorrows are horrible to this day. I am still stunned how well equipped the Nazis were in dealing with the realities of slave labor and genocide and I couldn't believe in my research and reading how another Ivan the Terrible appeared again in history. There was an Ivan the Terrible in Nazi Germany. This Ivan the Terrible after World War 2 settled in the suburbs of Cleveland with his wife and children. I found this ironic as Cleveland is my hometown. It was hard for me to believe, in the spirit of understanding, that he was even allowed to come here after all that he did, killing and torturing so many Jews, although he denied it.

In the Holocaust Ivan the Terrible and Hitler seemed to regard the Nazi atrocities as a bunch of fun-and-games. Born in 1911, this Ivan the Terrible appears in history this time as a nickname given to the devil guard Ivan Marchenko at the Treblinka extermination camp. In 2011 he was accused of war crimes as a different guard called Ivan Demjanjuk who brutalized Jews and stoically sent them to the ovens. The upshot is it appears he was an accessory to the murders of about 27,900 Jews, his convictions always overturned. He died a free man and legally innocent.

I remember in my class listening to a concentration camp survivor give a lecture. He gave the most inspiring speech I have ever heard. It gave me powerful motivation to want to protect people from this kind of thing even though I knew very sadly that horrors are so difficult to prevent from taking place. I couldn't believe what I was hearing when this concentration camp survivor spoke. He told us as much as he could about the dehumanization and how it began immediately, and how the Jews quickly lost their emotions. He went on to explain that the Jews in Germany were too passive and just went with their yellow stars on their clothes and reported to the death camps. They went quietly, and the Germans seemed to know that the Jews wouldn't fight. It seems as if the Jews were in shock about it all and couldn't believe that it was happening. They were in a daze and didn't begin to fight back and form an underground until much later in the war after so many died.

I remember the concentration camp survivor went on to say that today's Jews are not like yesterday's Jews. Today's Jews have a different response to attacks and abuse. I still recall in the gentleman's lecture he pointed out that today's Jew will fight. If, you hit him in the left cheek he will hit you harder in your right cheek. That new attitude is why in Israel women and men serve in the military. Whoever attacks anyone in Israel, the entire country immediately goes on the offensive, women and men, old and young alike. Whoever can fight will fight. Everyone is trained. The entire nation will strike back with a vengeance.

Popular consciousness must catch up with the crimes committed against humankind just because of their culture. My Holocaust Jewish Professor marched with Dr. Martin Luther King during the civil rights marches. African Americans and Jews have a lot in common in all they have had to contend with in history. It is hurtful. Popular consciousness must catch up with the crimes committed against all people, all of humanity. The grim wartime atrocities of the Holocaust will be remembered. There are lessons to be learned from history, but my question is will people learn from them?

My class taught me a lot about hate-propaganda. There is no doubt that it precedes and accompanies ethnic and religious conflicts. Criminal hate speeches are dangerous and are destructive messages and pave the way for group hatred. We must openly address hatred if we are to protect public peace. How many people does it take to die until the climate of hated stops? It saddens me that hate is seen in posters, films and exhibits. It is seen in in article writing and in books and on television and is daily in the news. There is only one thing that can be done and that is all people must work together, collectively to stop hate and its effectiveness.

The liberty bells of freedom
Ring for all~

Luis Cumba

CHAPTER NINE

President Lincoln was a prime example of standing out from the crowd. I don't believe there has been any other American so widely commemorated as him. I wonder if her was here what he would say to today's Americans about race and freedom and the justice we are all seeking. I wonder what his thoughts would be on the race relations and culture divisions that face this country today. No doubt he struggled tirelessly with the pain of leadership.

I have read the rare printed materials, original manuscripts, listened to audiobooks, attended library exhibits and museum attractions to study President Lincoln and civil rights. Under his presidency I have studied democracy, freedom Lincoln's government and economic opportunities under his presidency. I have studied everything under the sun that has had a connection to Lincoln and I have concluded that President Lincoln was a model and champion to all Americans and to the world. Slavery played the central role during the American Civil War and it plays a central role in the world today.

President Abraham Lincoln fought very hard to abolish slavery and I studied him like there was no tomorrow at school. The truth being that I am a history buff and found President Lincoln to be one of the finest personalities in the history of the United States. He has been read in books, seen in movies, discussed in articles and his historical accounts have been selected by an array of politicians who made his stand part of their political promises. Lincoln has become America's champion, America's hero in its fight against bigotry. But with all that President Lincoln managed to do, it wasn't until the 1960's when civil rights movements started all over the nation with the Kennedy's and Dr. Martin Luther King changing the pages of history with the struggle. All three of them champions, President Kennedy, his brother Robert Kennedy and Dr. Martin Luther King all killed by an assassin's bullet.

I remember thinking that America's attitude about racism must change and so I studied President Lincoln Every second I got, I was researching and reading the history of America. I couldn't get enough of it. I couldn't get enough of the research that I was doing. I must admit I grew very emotional as I grew to admire President Lincoln. Talk about someone who had so much on his plate. Not only was he contending with slavery, he was dealing with his wife's mental illness issues. He never lost hope for the nation. My study of the past and my focus on historical accuracy has contributed to my status as a Civil Rights Expert.

I buried my head in so much reading material just like I did with the Holocaust, but I read it all with zeal and passion. Remember, dear reader, as a police officer all the way up to Captain, I always wanted to be the best. I have always wanted to make life better for. But what I didn't realize was that my excursions into the past, particularly those that took up American racism and racial violence would contribute to my effectiveness as a Police Captain for the fine city of Cleveland. And I know I am getting ahead of myself but the advancements in my life take me back to my solitary moments of reading about slavery and President Abraham Lincoln which I will share with you now.

I remember I was working a political event in an all-black district in Cleveland. Dressed in my police uniform, word got out out at the event that I was a Police Captain. Now, as a Captain, I never sat behind my desk. I was always very active in the community so people could see me and recognize me. I wanted to break down the barriers and be approachable despite my high ranking of Police Captain. A few children came up to me and said right to my face that they hated the police. I was taken aback, but only for a second for I then realized they were taught this and perhaps they were taught this because someone in their family or a friend had experienced a bad experience with the police.

I made sure as Police Captain I increased the number of women and minorities into the Cleveland Police Department. I felt that women police bring special qualities and attributes into the police department. In policing, gender integration brings opportunity for women to participate in forming policy and bringing betterment to the department. The police role for women was established because of their determination and struggle.

I just made sure that on my watch the doors were open to women in the Cleveland Police Department and I did my best to make sure they were trained properly and succeeded. I believe that acceptance by their male peers is still in the making. Today acceptance by the public has grown as female police officers have been seen more frequently on the street on patrol and in uniform. Despite racist slurs, policies and behaviors in the department, I also opened the door and encouraged minorities into the Cleveland Police Department saying there is no color in the department except blue. If everyone is "blue enough" then they are welcome into the department. As long as they had what it took to be a great cop they were welcome. And, under my watch there was room for advancement for all.

As a police officer on the streets, a police sergeant, lieutenant and captain, I studied criminal motives and behavior and the various possibilities of reforming criminals and making them positive citizens and transition them from their life of crime. There is no doubt that crime is a major part of society's fabric and armed robbery and killing is the result of the crime in many cases. As a cop I learned to see the relationship between crime in the cities and everyday life. Crime impacts cities and impacts human beings in every walk of life. People all over the world have different opinions of theft. Perhaps they know someone who is a thief or are related to somebody who in imprisoned for stealing. Opinions are very diverse about crime whoever you talk to. As a cop who ever since he was a child as you know had dreams of protecting and serving, I have always felt it was right to bust those who steal and as a cop I did just that. But that does not mean that I didn't then and don't now believe in doing more. Reform is doing more not doing less. The various categories of crime and violent thefts as felonies and different crimes constitute different offences and come along with different punishments.

Everything always depends on circumstances, the values of the items stolen and the circumstances that surround the crimes. There is always so much to consider. And so, I would bury my head and read. Exceptional criminal activity created sensational highly publicized stories of crimes and crime enactments and I read the high-profile cases and studied them all. Pickpocketing and burglary, breaking into someone's home, extortion, shoplifting and so on all have their own brand attached to them. Receiving stolen goods goes into the mix as well.

When I decided to become a police officer I did it in the spirit of profound love, strength and compassion. And when I think about my life as a cop, it allows me to travel back in time to remember moments of my childhood. Such riveting things like my concerns for kindness and that children should be counted even though they are just little kids. My parents always were there to listen what each of my siblings had to say and they made us feel important. I always felt that people and children and animals and the elderly should be counted for being living beings and that their life matters. My zeal for genuine compassion for all was powerful. And I wanted people to know that they were liked just as they were and not how society thought they should be. I know that this came to me from my young childhood days in Puerto Rico.

It is also essential to understand the reason I decided to become a police officer. I had wanted to be in law enforcement for so long. I was armed with my beliefs and those beliefs were in my heart, soul and mind. What I didn't have any idea of was that I would become a bona fide American hero and tireless public servant. I pursued equality in everything I did because I wanted to make the world right and I knew that although it was just a small part of life, I felt that I wanted to carry out law enforcement in a way that would make Lincoln proud.

I just knew I wanted to be a cop to try to make things better. That's all I knew. But I have always been a very motivated person and a high achiever from a very young age. Ever since I was born, I was a person who would dream big and I've kept that dream gene in me alive and well throughout my life. Honestly, I think I was born with the dream gene. I would daydream as well as dream at night and always felt that my dreams told me something. I always saw the same thing, running after love to make the world better and as a policeman, I would be on the tail of love and catch it and somehow make the world surrender to it! I was going to make the world love and make people love one another. I wanted the world to feel the love vibe.

I think my dreams made me feel courageous. I did not like the feeling of fear. If an alarm sounded I would want to check it out. If a car plummeted down an embankment and was embedded in a circle of red flashing lights, I wanted to be the fireman or the policeman to disengage someone from the wreckage. I wanted to rescue people. I wanted to be that guy who was not afraid to jump in and do something to help. It didn't matter if it was someone darting from an alley screaming for help or if I was running a sick feverish friend to a clinic, I wanted to make it all right and be a first line responder to disaster situations. I was quick on my feet and a fast runner and ready to help. I wanted to help. I have always been the type of person who says what am I going to give, not what am I going to get. I never had that needy energy of what am I going to get if I do this or that. And this is what makes me who I am, this and my God.

Somehow from a very young age, I've learned not to panic. Maybe that is because I always felt God in everything that I have ever done. I have always felt that together people can do something, too. We as a people can do everything! So, I am a proactive person, but reactive in situations. I will jump into a situation as I have said to make it better. But, I am proactive in the respect I will go out of my way to make something happen. I admire people who don't sit around and complain or blame anyone. In this world you must make your own opportunities and create your own path and not make yourself a victim.

And so, I decided to give life my best shot like my parents taught me to do. I joined the Cleveland Police Academy and in no time, I was the fastest riser in the police force. I excelled in academics, fitness and shooting and became number one in my platoon. I trained very hard and I studied hard. I think that my entry-level fitness was really the crystal ball of predicting my subsequent police academy success. I was fast at everything. Learning and running came easy to me. I loved it all. Everything being a police officer delighted me and I did well at it. In no time I memorized every law and knew what everything meant.

I loved what I was learning, and I learned it fast. But I knew that there was a psychological part of being a cop along with the physical side of it. Law enforcement included many stressors. Would I be able to handle the frequent overtime, the low decisional control (everything was an order from a superior that I had to follow) and could I do the shift work and how would I be in the frequent confrontational situations that I would be in with people that may not be rationale. I decided that I would make myself great at it all and I did because in the end, I knew I was great at doing useful things.

I was great at physical exertion. I was fast on my feet and a quick thinker. The rigorous training regimen at the Academy is meant to instill pride and discipline in each recruit and I had the stamina to succeed from the start. I had the power to stay on top. You learn early on to respect the chain of command. And training was tough. It was tough on the mind and tough on the feet, but I loved every single moment of it. Training included academia, enforcement tactics, physical training, vehicle operations and weapons training. All of it was very important and essential to being, a well-informed and well-trained officer. Police are trained to enforce the law based on our constitution. That is what it is about. Police don't make the laws, they enforce the laws. Cops need to stick to the principles of the Constitution. It is only in this way can things be right, and the public know and realize that police enforce the law. Still and all history makes people bitter.

I knew if I was going to join the police force I was going to have to accept those rules. People are bitter, and history makes us bitter. And this is very hard for police to work in a bitter and angry environment. But, it will continue to be this way. Everyone will see each other as human. My life in Puerto Rico taught me how important it was to live in peace with all races and all religions. I was raised in this way. I was raised to love everyone. Puerto Rico is a place that lives in peace with whites black and Indians and this is the way we were raised. That's the way we were brought up to love everyone and like everyone. I'm just Lou. I'm a regular American. I get along with everyone. I was raised in Long Island and got along with everyone and I brought this to my training at the police academy.

As a kid in my junior high school days, I would see cars parked along the curb and it gave me a great appreciation of what police officers faced everyday being in a marked car. A policeman's uniform and patrol car were all anyone needed to attack him or her and so I knew, if I were going to become a cop, I had to be good at protecting not only the public but myself as well. And that is why understanding the academics of the job came so easily to me because I understood the need for it, the rationale behind the Constitution and what my job was as a police officer. A police officer's role was not to gain power but to participate in the fight for public welfare. A police officer is there to enforce the law for the good of all people to make them safe and so people can enjoy justice, freedom, fairness. Promises should not be broken and should not come from a barrel of a gun. People easily become suspicious, confused, angry and disappointed. My job was to make sure that these feelings did not erupt on the streets and turn the city of Cleveland into a violent one and I didn't want to be a police officer in a city of bulldozers pushing rubble.

*A stream of literature is devoted to
saying crime doesn't pay
But crime continues to chug along
and is America's biggest train wreck~*

Luis Cumba

I was born protective. I always wanted to be a policeman, to protect and serve. My family came to the US Mainland from Puerto Rico when I was a little and I would begin school on the Mainland. As soon as I could, I lived my dream and more. I am a proud Puerto Rican American, Retired Firefighter, Wild Fire Expert and Police Captain from the beautiful city of Cleveland Ohio. I am a Civil Rights Expert, a First Responder and an expert in Civil Rights Disaster, Riot Control, Civil Disorder, Homeland Security, Internal Affairs Investigation, Police Brutality and SWAT Command Specialist where along with my team we built the best SWAT department in Cleveland and the country. My job was to use the finest equipment and save lives. Yes. I have lived my dream and more. I have always tried to live up to my potential and push myself beyond my potential.

Luis Cumba

CHAPTER TEN

I never struggled to wrap my mind around the magnitude of the job of being a policeman. I knew there was a lot to it. I knew there was going to take a lot of me to be a policeman. But I also knew that I was ready for the commitment. And so, what I did was just dive into the business and the training and the whole deal of becoming a cop. I took it on like you wouldn't believe. I became obsessed with it all. I was obsessed with the training and the studying. I was involved in every aspect of everything, equally. I never studied one thing more than the other. I put a big grin on my face, built up a great rapport with everyone in the department and learned everything from the gun belt to the police flashlight to the armor to the police radio which was communication and provided contact with the department's dispatch office.

I knew the laws and every part of everything that I needed to know. I learned about the Blue Coats Award. The Blue Coats Award was a foundation founded by men and women. It was put together for a policeman's family. If anything were to ever happen to a police officer or a cop was killed in the line of duty, then this foundation would take care of the cop's family. The foundation would send a cop's kids to school and pay off all the bills.

I am proud to say that I was at the top in my class. As a policeman, I worked hard all the time and I made a lot of arrests. I always made between three and five arrests a day and distributed about fifteen tickets every day. On my night shift one night, I remember my patrol car was the only car working the west side district and it was my patrol car that responded to everything and I was patrolling the entire responding to crime. The Lieutenant was aware of this and liked me. He saw that I was young and filled with a lot of potential. He could tell I liked my job. He's the one that allowed me to take the promotional test and I made Sergeant in two and a half years. I studied hard for the next test and I studied for six months ten to twelve hours a day. I made this after four years. No one has ever done that. And so, the Cumba rule was put together which basically said you cannot take another promotion until you've served in a certain position for two years.

I was a Police Sergeant for less than a year. I spent most of my time studying for the next rank. I was very ambitious, but I was born ambitious. I went to great lengths to succeed. I have always been known for my drive to succeed, my independence and my loyalty to people, a cause and to an office. Everything I have ever done in life and my career in law enforcement has been achieved because I don't believe in setting limits. I see the greater possibilities in everything I do because I take everything I do seriously. I set no limits for myself. I believe that you must feel the potential you have, and you've got to believe in yourself. Everything I did and do in life is done with discipline, commitment and sincerity. And so, I made Police Sergeant after two years. I knew the law hands down and studied the evidence of a crime night and day. I never overlooked a thing. Always being brave, I never allowed my fears to interpret evidence or distort or influence what I saw. I knew what I saw, and I proudly stood by it.

It wasn't long after I became a policeman that the higher ups noticed me. They saw that I was a smart officer and that I had a lot of potential. I was young, in great shape and educated. I caught on to things quickly. I respected authority. My disposition was remarkable in every situation and the higher ups noticed this as well. However bad life seemed, I always felt there was something I could do to make a change and make things better and the higher ups saw this positive attitude in me and they liked it. I soared to the top of the lists and defined myself by my ability to overcome the impossible. I achieved.

The moments when I dared to reach higher was really my hallmark in life. I was out to break the barriers. Clearly, I was career-focused and asked all the right questions. I also listened to the right answers and mastered them and let them guide me. What resonated with me was doing the right things and going beyond my capabilities. A steady paycheck wasn't enough for me. It wasn't the answer. I had to go beyond my achievements. I wanted to be able to pay my bills and live nicely and live in the kind of house that I dreamed of and I do now, to this day. I live in what I called the mansion! When I look back at life, I attained my dream. Yes! I live in the kind of house that I always dreamed of and everyone in the neighborhood calls my residence the *mansion*, not only because it is beautiful but because it is comfortable, welcoming and friendly. When kids are walking down the street they always come up to me when I am outside and tell me how much they love my house! It makes me feel warm inside.

I have often thought why I decided to become a policeman. There were many reasons. I think back to when I got the notion to be one and a few situations come to mind. Prejudice. Prejudice comes to mind. Bigotry is ignorance and has long prevailed among people on this planet since the beginning of time and Long Island New York in the 1970s sticks in my mind once again as I write this chapter in my life. The notion, the thought, the realization of not being free was a big part for me wanting to become a policeman and it takes me back to my own dealing with prejudice. Remember as I mentioned earlier, I got hit with prejudice as a young guy. Yes.

I was Luis Cumba a Hispanic in Long Island in the 1970s and that has stayed in my mind all these years. It mirrors humanity at its worst in my mind. There is no doubt that existing prejudice creates bitterness and calls to mind that no one is imperfect because of their ethnicity. There is also no doubt that one of the chief factors in life today is the strengthening of prejudice and the bitterness it creates. The world is filled with a jumble of bigotry and my own dealings with it has stayed in my mind and became a big motivating force for me to succeed as a cop and change things. Remember, I always have wanted to change the world!

Even today, after all these years later, I am startled and surprised and horrified by bigotry. What in the heck is wrong with people? We could all be more if we could be one people. Still to this day when I think about my own experiences with prejudice it I am filled with a shudder of horror and disappointment for society. I wasn't the product of some alien civilization. But that is what it seemed like. I was just a guy from Puerto Rico! And you know how certain things stay in your memory for life? I still remember being stopped driving to church driving someone else's car and I completely forgot about the ticket that was in the car because it wasn't my car and I got stopped for that and razzed. I have never been slowed down by bigotry, it has only made me try harder.

Today, most officers are better educated. Brutality is closely monitored in major cities and the brutality itself are in urban areas within their community. I worked in internal affairs for 16 years and reviewed over 6000 cases and was filled with so much horror over it all. Racism is distorted and diabolical. People learn so soon in their lives to hate instinctively. It's all mad and silly and foolish and meaningless. Sometimes, I would find myself burying my head in my arms over it all. It was so sad to know that bigotry has become a way of life and to know that I wasn't the only one experiencing it. Through the blinding tears of racism, I felt then as much as now the regret and condolence that dims peoples vision over an individual just because of their race, culture and religion.

I couldn't have done anything in the slightest degree that was dishonorable or far less anything wicked than arrest someone for being Hispanic or Jewish or Black, etc. Racism is this horrible, mysterious, known barrier that raises its ugly head in situations and makes people hate one another. there. Racism has its own shock. The sanest more clear-headed people admit how troubling racism is. The mocking grimaces, the snide remarks, the disrespect is hard to stomach. I realize you must rationalize the attention bigotry brings to people and you must understand that those who are prejudiced have madness on the brain. They are angry people.

I want all people to be treated equally like the Constitution says and as a cop, it was always my goal to treat all people equally and broaden the department with women and minorities which I did. Serving the public and protecting the public, everyone, in the same way was very important to me. And I must admit, my thoughts on racism could complete a second volume because bigotry is an act of injustice. I will always try to wipe off the earth.

My motivation to get into law enforcement and succeed is who I am. Proudly, I made Sergeant in three years, Lieutenant in four years and Captain after eleven years. I thank my mother and father for instilling the values in me that they did and for making me every accomplishment that I ever was. And I thank my God for keeping me safe and being by my side.

Community involvement
Shows law enforcement at its best~

Luis Cumba

CHAPTER ELEVEN

I have always believed that the police should maintain a philosophy of community involvement. The old system of policing does not cope well with the community. For me to be an effective arm of the law the community must see cops as helpful not hurtful. It starts with the kids on the streets. They must see police smile and shake hands and give holiday gifts and attend events. The police must be part of the community they patrol.

New techniques for maintain community peace must be created. I personally developed relationships with the community. I was out there at every level of my police career out on the streets. I always made sure to stress the need for law enforcement to create and develop relationships with the elderly, children, teens and parents that was based on respect. If you can show respect for the community, you will receive trust. It is all about communication. Establishing communication is a must.

Communication, good communication establishes peace. Good communication with the community leads to crime reduction and implements police accountability. Effective communication with the community leads to a feeling of police partnering with the community and this is what I used to do. I partnered with the community in my efforts to gain trust and promote peace. It is all about crime reduction, handling protests effectively and creating a prevalent attitude
that unfolds a practice of understanding and patience.

Community policing is critical, and it is the path to police being responsible to community needs. Police must understand the art of policing. I never wanted people to be afraid of me because I was a cop. I wanted to establish a huge reach into the community and this was able to take place because I always made myself accountable to the people. The people are who I protected as a cop and so I should be accountable to the people. This was my motto. It was always about resolving disputes peacefully if possible and being responsive to the community.

It is about protection and justice and equality, Perspective must change on both sides. Local leaders must also establish community communication and they must visit the people and not police from a desk. I never policed from my desk. I was out there in the community being the face to hear diverse views. Police partnering with the community has everything to do with problem-solving. Police absolutely must stand on a platform of sincerity and over again I say that the police must reassure the community.

Effectiveness was what I was always about when I served in law enforcement. It was important for me to serve my profession and practice a de-escalation protocol. Bringing peace to the community was my goal in everything I did. Community policing is a good as the police that serve that community. Police are essential. Gaining the trust of the community you are protecting is essential too. Partnering with the community and gaining trust from all walks of life comes from giving respect. Giving respect is the most effective way of gaining respect. I was proud to serve with my brothers and sisters in blue and save and protect lives.

First Responders Are Yesterday's Heroes
Tomorrow's Heroes
Everyday Heroes
And Everyone's Heroes~

Luis Cumba

First responders brave the dangerous flames of fire. They are on the scene of terrorism. They respond to everything and dedicate their lives to protecting others. They always respond first and are there to help and to comfort and many lose their life in the line of duty. They train hard and they move fast. They cope with the intensity that is thrown at them and they are trained in the most advanced first aid skills known to humankind. Everything they do is to save lives. In moments that test our faith, they emerge. They are truly our heroes.

First responders see things that the public cannot even fathom. Floods, fires, earthquakes, hurricanes, tornados, school shootings, crashes and every horror story you can think of first responders experience. They rush into danger and their typical day is filled with the most outlandish scenarios.
I have been honored to serve with them and proudly salute them.

Luis Cumba

CHAPTER TWELVE

First responders go through intensive training, training that the average person cannot even attempt to imagine and why is this? I will tell you. Disasters always happen. They can occur anywhere and at anytime and first responders must be ready and must be prepared because, unfortunately, communities are not. First responders effectively respond to all types of disasters. They are trained for this and they are trained to effectively handle crisis situations. I salute every single first responder. Each one of them is unique, gifted and the best!

I've made a lot of friends along the way as a firefighter, first responder and a member of law enforcement at every level. I have learned that police officers receive a lot of respect from all division of the community when police are trained properly from their department and work with others. **I have been trained properly. I was a trained Swat Commander and in the days before the massacre at Columbine High School, they called SWAT and when first responders arrived they waited until they had enough people to go in. It has all changed since April 20, 1999 when** Columbine High School in Littleton, Colorado entered the picture. Two teens when on a shooting spree, twelve students were murdered, and one teacher and 21 additional people were injured while attempting to escape the high school before the two teens turned their guns on themselves and committed suicide. It changed the nation.

Columbine sparked debate over our gun control laws and school security policies. I can comment on this. If armed police who are first responders arrive and immediately go into the situation and it is a panic situation and a police officer sees anyone, who is armed they are going to go down. So, arming teachers will not work. Teachers, students and anyone who is armed will go down when the police get on the scene. In an out-of-control situation, a police officer is going to protect those unarmed against those armed.

I remember it was decided one very early morning that if we have a school shooting (after Columbine) that first responders go to the scene immediately. In other words, we get the call, we go. It is as simple as that. We go in regardless of weaponry. We are going in with one goal in mind and that is to save lives. We are not going to wait for any back up. Now, in a situation like this the first thing that you must do is mentally and physically prepare. Preparing makes you stronger, faster and smarter in what you are going to be facing. First responders who are well-prepared have the peace of mind to concentrate on the task at hand. Focus is essential and having clarity is of utmost importance to be effective. First responders are the human story from beginning to end in any disaster situation. First responders are the first to meet the human face and see the suffering.

As a cop I can tell you there is no such thing
As a routine crime adventure~

Luis Cumba

During the course of my journey as a police officer I've experienced many realities of American life, such as fast-talking con-artists eager to give me money in exchange for favors, thugs eager to take lives for the hell of it as well as see with my own eyes the disparity between the rich and poor, and the existence of black slavery, Black and Hispanic and female discrimination and the probing questions involving contradictions of democracy in American society. In other words, I've seen a lot in my career as a police officer. I've done a lot in my life including die.

Luis Cumba

My prevailing perspective on street drug abuse derived from many things. But one thing to really keep in mind is that I was a Lieutenant in the Cleveland Police Department and I can tell you we did not just bust people for no reason. That is not what we stood for. We knew too well what revealed the ideological forces that shape the nature of street-addict life. We also knew the hard-core drug users and their dope friends that were really fiends that haunted the city streets. We had dramatic, first-person accounts of Cleveland addicts. We knew too well all the drugs that were filtering in and out of Cleveland.

Luis Cumba

CHAPTER THIRTEEN

The mean streets of Cleveland are something I will never forget. They played host to an evil underworld of addicts and pushers and junkies and everything else. We met every type of ruthless unsavory character and it made me sick. I always wanted to try to make things better, but it is very hard to clean up the streets. I tried to make it a personal fight to bust violent rings of heroin, coke, and smack and dope dealers during a turbulent era in the city's history but I've got to admit, it was difficult. It was very difficult, and it saddened me. I was a tough cop but there were times I was very effected by it all, especially if there were young people involved. It always bothered me when young people were ruining their lives on the streets.

My years on the inside of the Cleveland Police Department makes me reflect on many things, but my days trying to infiltrate the criminal drug world through narc-sharing and my personal observations on personal peril and ruined lives because of drug trading really had me reach a bump in the road because there was no set cure to make it all better. If I had to I was always willing to punch my way out of trouble. But, the drug war was a 24 hour and seven day a week job and you still couldn't make a dent in it. We did all sorts of drug raids where we caught the pushers and junkies by surprise but there were still drugs and more drugs on the streets. Even if we got the junkie stool pigeons to talk and the hooker informants and the gang burnouts who were tired of being thugs and wanted refuge and protection in exchange for their information we met with bureaucratic obstacles and so on. We weren't just dealing with our country and red tape we were dealing with foreign governments and their role in drug trafficking. And there were a lot of uncooperative foreign governments.

Pot, coke, acid, amphetamines always made my life difficult as I tried to implement our surprise drug raids, but you couldn't break the cycle of those seeking the ultimate high. That ultimate high is what ruined the streets of Cleveland and what created Cleveland's major drug problem that was ruining the great city and resulting in the long nights, sudden danger, and uncertain outcomes that faced us in our efforts to clean up the streets. I'm going to admit right here that my face was changing. I was still young and good looking and filled with ambition, but the tired lines around my eyes were capturing the futility that was filling my days and creating the endless frustration I was experiencing. I was a cop, and I hated violence, I didn't like having to shoot anyone.

The war on drugs gave me a window in the harsh world of illegal drugs on the streets and I kept that picture on my mind well beyond our debriefings and well beyond when the SWAT guys were going in to raid a place that we expected something was going to happen. We raided so many houses for drugs. 450 and 600 drugs raids in one year on my watch and under my direction. There were lots and lots of drug activity. Tons of kilos of cocaine. I remained mentally and physically and emotionally strong to clean up the streets. And at the end of the day, after every major incident, I would get together with the guys, my fellow police officers that were under me and we would critique how it went and see if we both liked it. I believed we had to learn from everything and see if there was a better way of doing it all. The key to life is making it all better. And that is what I tried to do every day I was a cop.

I want to say a few things here. Being a cop made me realize something and that is meeting high expectations and performing tasks that involved protecting and serving was what I was all about. I saw the light when I was a cop. And, although I was shy by nature, the protective part of me gave me a place for feelings of, hope, excitement and worth and really has always seemed to occupy my journey. Being a cop really completed me as a person. I knew it was the right career for me.

The other thing is that since I was a little kid God and I were joined at the hip. I have always had a tendency toward resolution and being a problem solver. I didn't believe in settling problems with my fists, but I wouldn't walk away from a fist fight either, if I believed in it. I was very sympathetic as a child and other people and their feelings always mattered to me. I tried to look at everything realistically and remain ultimately hopeful in every experience I encountered, and this emerged even more as a cop.

I always wanted to be a policeman. When I made Captain, it was no easy thing. I I really busted my butt to be something that I really wanted to be. The greatest thing in my life was my mother was with me when I made Captain, and this really added to my accomplishment in law enforcement. The fact that my mother saw me achieve was the height of my career and has been the height of my life. She died a year later. She got to see it though. She got to see me promoted. I was deeply grateful she was there. Having her there with me was an honor for me, one of the greatest honors of my life. Yes. Mom and I were very close. I was very much a mama's boy. I was her favorite. My brothers and sisters say that to this day. Everyone in the family knew it. Having her there while I was presented with my degree brings tears to my eyes right now.

I was the first person in my family to get a college degree and it was also a momentous occasion for me. Becoming Police Captain was a great thing. It was something that I wanted to do. Everyone who knew me knew how I took my career seriously. I wanted to be the best and I succeeded in it. Yes. I proudly served the people of Cleveland. I was proud to stand with my brothers and sisters in blue and I was proud of my accomplishments as a police officer and be among America's first responders and their heroics. They are, indeed, America's heroes.

CHAPTER FOURTEEN

When I decided to become a cop, I didn't have any idea that I would become a bona fide American hero and tireless public servant. I just knew I wanted to be a cop. That's all I knew. I had no idea about SWAT. I had no idea that I would grow up to be SWAT Commander of Cleveland either. I was just a little kid, a protective little kid who was highly motivated and a high achiever from a very young age. Ever since I was born, I was a person who would dream big and I've kept that dream gene in me alive and well throughout my life. Honestly, I think I was born with the dream gene. I would daydream and dream at night and always felt that my dreams told me something.

I had no fear. If an alarm sounded I would want to check it out. If a car plummeted down an embankment and embedded in a circle of red flashing lights, I wanted to be the fireman or the policeman to disengage someone from the wreckage. I wanted to rescue people. I wanted to be that guy who was not afraid to jump into it all. It didn't matter if it was someone darting from an alley screaming for help or if I was running a sick feverish friend to the hospital, I wanted to make it right and be a first line responder to disaster situations. I was quick on my feet and a fast runner and ready to help. I wanted to help. I wanted to make things better. I have always been the type of guy who says what am I going to give, not what am I going to get. And this is what makes me who I am, this and my God.

Somehow from a very young age, I've learned not to panic. Maybe that is because I always felt God in everything that I have ever done. I have always felt that together people can do something, too. We as a people can do everything! So, I am a proactive person, but reactive in situations. I will jump into a situation as I have said to make it better.

But, I am proactive in the respect I will go out of my way to make something happen. I admire people who don't sit around and complain or blame anyone. In this world you must make your own opportunities and create your own path.

The mean streets of Cleveland are something I will never forget. They played host to an evil underworld of addicts and pushers and junkies and everything else. We met every type of ruthless unsavory character and it made me sick. I always wanted to try to make things better, but it was very hard to clean up the streets. I tried, along with my brothers and sisters in blue to bust up the violent rings of heroin, coke, and smack and dope dealers, but I must admit, it was difficult. It was very difficult, and it saddened me. I was a tough cop but there were times I was overwhelmed by it all, especially if there were young people involved. It always bothered me when young people were ruining their lives on the streets.

My years on the inside of the Cleveland Police Department makes me reflect on many things, but my days trying to infiltrate the criminal drug world through narc-sharing and my personal observations on personal peril and ruined lives because of drug trading really had me reach a bump in the road because there was no set cure to make it all better. If I had to I was always willing to punch my way out of trouble. But, the drug war was a 24 hour and seven day a week job and you still couldn't make a dent in it. We did all sorts of drug raids where we caught the pushers and junkies by surprise but there were still drugs and more drugs on the streets. Even if we got the junkie stool pigeons to talk and the hooker informants and the gang burnouts who were tired of being thugs and wanted refuge and protection in exchange for their information we met with bureaucratic obstacles and so on. We weren't just dealing with our country and red tape we were dealing with foreign governments and their role in drug trafficking. And there were a lot of uncooperative foreign governments.

Pot, coke, acid, amphetamines always made my law enforcement life difficult as I tried to implement our surprise drug raids, but you couldn't break the cycle of those seeking the ultimate high. That ultimate high is what ruined the streets of Cleveland and what created Cleveland's major drug problem that was ruining the great city and resulting in the long nights, sudden danger, and uncertain outcomes that faced us in our efforts to clean up the streets. I'm going to admit right here that my face was changing. I was still young and good looking and filled with ambition, but the tired lines around my eyes were capturing the futility that was filling my days and creating the endless frustration I was experiencing.

I was a cop, and I hated violence, I didn't like having to shoot anyone. The war on drugs gave me a window in the harsh world of illegal drugs on the streets and I kept that picture on my mind well beyond our debriefings and well beyond when the SWAT guys were going in to raid a place that we expected something was going to happen. We raided so many houses for drugs. 450 and 600 drugs raids in one year on my watch and under my direction. There were lots and lots of drug activity. Tons of kilos of cocaine. I remained mentally and physically and emotionally strong to clean up the streets. And at the end of the day, after every major incident, I would get together with the guys, my fellow police officers that were under me and we would critique how it went and see if we both liked it. I believed we had to learn from everything and see if there was a better way of doing it all.

And then came S.W.A.T.

SWAT was tough
And I was Going TO Make Sure It Stayed That way
In Cleveland ~

Luis Cumba

Cocaine and heroin raids were being conducted all over the nation. It was a high priority in every police department. Police officers were making drugs raids jumping out of the back of police vans like in the movies and storming homes and apartment buildings and pouring into backyards. Heavily armed cops would emerge at day break or break into bedrooms in the middle of the night, kick open the doors and arrest drug lords and leaders in their boxers and apprehend women in their negligees who were busy flushing their stash down toilets. The oftentimes trend of military-style operations targeting the drug world really took off on my watch in SWAT, my focus being the beautiful city of Cleveland~

Luis Cumba

Handling high risk situations effectively
Has changed the climate of crime.
It is called S.W.A.T.

Luis Cumba

CHAPTER FIFTEEN

We read these headlines often. SWAT officers prepare for armed standoff. SWAT Team surrounds armed murder suspect who has barricaded himself in an apartment building. Suspect believed to be fully armed and dangerous. SWAT armed with strong negotiating skills moved in with a team that is the finest and talks with suspect. SWAT clears the building and apprehends suspect. SWAT (Special Weapons and Tactics) team is a law enforcement unit of special marksmen shooters and negotiating experts implemented to neutralize situations so they don't lead to further tragedy and loss of life. SWAT had broken the mold of law enforcement and it was making headlines all over the nation. Ohio wanted to learn more about this new law enforcement force in Los Angeles and bring this knowledge back to Cleveland and the higher-ups decided that I was the guy to do it. I went out on my own dime to Los Angeles to see what it was all about.

My studies of criminology and theories of crime were very useful for me. I studied a lot about police behavior and I will tell you that appropriate behavior in any job is essential for effectiveness and for being on top of your job. Understanding criminal behavior is relevant as it enables us to draw the public in more positively and teaches us how to handle ourselves in the most dangerous of neighborhoods.

We can't turn our back on indifference and apathy and we can't erase the deaths that have happened. We must take measures to skillfully deal with every issue from every area and from every culture. Only then can we be at our best to be effective, stamp our hate and treat all people equally. I have done my best to uphold these truths that I believe in. I did my best to live up to the badge and have a career where I could make a difference in people's lives and make things better for all.

It never has left my mind how I made Sergeant in three years,

Lieutenant in four years and Captain after eleven years. I thank my mother and father for instilling the values in me that they did and for making me every accomplishment that I ever was. And I thank my God for keeping me safe and being by my side. I was honored to undertake these positions and I was elated and always ready for the next step up. I read and studied up on literally everything police related that I could get my hands on because I didn't want to be ineffective at executing anything or coping with anything. I never stopped giving my current responsibilities my all and I took every step of being a policeman very seriously and gave it everything I had. I also learned that patience was my friend and constant companion and that being responsive was the name of the game.

Every incident I was ever involved in I tried to execute without casualties. Dealing with crazies was difficult. I tried to mix in with the neighborhood as a cop. I was a great patrol officer that way. You had to out-guess the crazies and what better way to do that then to be among them. There is no doubt that the investigative nature of policing and the dangerous occupational environment in which police officers work, are believed to reinforce an attitude of suspiciousness toward both members of the public and even new colleagues. Sometimes this suspiciousness can reflect work habits. I learned that I had to balance things and not react emotionally and make sure that fairness was always practiced by me and enforced in the department.

I had a great memory and when officers used to ask me for citation numbers of a certain event, for any case and for any ticket I knew it. If it was a citation number for an unauthorized U turn, I knew it. I was respected and trusted by those I worked with and those who worked for me. Crazy things were always happening, and it didn't just have to be by the crazies. I remember it was 1984 and I got laid off. Cops were getting laid off like crazy. In May of the same year I was called back to the department and promoted to sergeant. Just because I was laid off didn't mean I was passed over for a promotion. So, I put on my uniform, went back to the department and without a badge was sworn in and received my Sargant's badge.

Then the craziest thing happened, I was laid off again and a month later I was called back, and I got sent over to the E district in

Cleveland. Everyone saw how strong and tough I was. I studied my butt off again. After Sargant I got promoted in 1985 to Lieutenant. When I made Lieutenant in 1985---I aced the test. I did so well. I was put into internal affairs and that is when I was told I was in great shape and had a lot of potential and was told to interview with SWAT, and that is exactly what I did! I interviewed for the SWAT position and got it! I have always had cop in my veins and in my genes and now it was SWAT.

I can't quite explain it. I never liked wrong-doers. I always wanted to protect the innocent. And I was also fully aware of what the presence of a cop car does to a community. When I was a cop on my own beat I easily saw how when my car was seen on the street and how the atmosphere of a street or neighborhood changed. The energy and vitality of an entire neighborhood changes when a black and white unit takes a drive through the streets. There are strained relations with the public and the police and the way the police have handled incidents in the past are never devoid of retaliatory attacks.

When I came on the force, I wanted to help the good people in neighborhoods with the issues they had and certainly not make them worse and during my time on the force and even today as a retired cop still make it a priority to improve police relations with the community as I did back then. I had to be me on the job. I had to be me. I had to understand what was pivotal to the success of a new policy or procedure. It was important for me to be a role model and mentor to many and lead by example, not because it was my job but because it was how I believed. I wanted to convey the positive aspects of policies and take the tie to explain them so those I was leading could see how what we were implementing were a benefit to all. Only in this way, would policies be a success.

Once again, I'm just Lou. A proud Puerto Rican American who loves his God and served America and the streets of Cleveland alongside with his brothers and sisters in blue to make the streets safe in Cleveland and all over the country. Now on to SWAT and some of my police escapades, rescues and philosophies. I want to say one thing before moving on and that is SWAT not only has changed the way we handle tense situations, it has added to America's legacy and mine.

Everything I did as a police officer required physical strength and mental and physical flexibility. Mental flexibility is essential because in everything you do you have to be able to adapt to the situation. You never know what is going to happen and you must be mentally alert always. The one time that you are not you endanger yourself and those around you. It is part of the leadership role as a Police Captain, especially. You must stay mentally fit, searching for clues and discovering connections until the mystery of the case is finally solved. The process of building a case of making logical inferences from all the scattered clues is something that you have be on top of all the time, every time. If you get sloppy you could lose your life and endanger everyone involved. You have to be on your toes physically and mentally and you have to be emotionally fit as well and I was from the very first moment I put on my uniform.

I really felt the mental, physical and emotional fitness in my job as SWAT Commander. My first incident that I responded to as a SWAT Commander (Special Weapons and Tactics Team) was a male barricaded in a house, shooting at the neighborhood. Now, SWAT Officers are specially trained to intervene in high-risk events like hostage and barricade situations and this situation involved a barricaded individual shooting up a neighborhood. From the moment we arrived (my team and I) and we could hear him shooting. The situation was disturbing and grim. I knew I had to make the right decision. I knew one thing off the bat that the gunman's destination was final unless he complied to our terms which were simple. Put down your gun and come out with your hands up type of a scenario. Ordinary citizens, who were part of society and composed a neighborhood were being shot at and the situation had to be neutralized. We were SWAT and we were not going to be ignored and we certainly were not going to abandon the neighborhood.

We were not going to go anywhere, and I think the criminal knew that. As we got closer to the shooter we found an empty room adjacent to his location. He continued shooting and ignoring our demands. He wouldn't come out even after we gassed him. We had no choice. We went in and he shot an entering member of our SWAT team. He had a big ballistic shield that protected him. We killed the suspect after he wouldn't stop shooting and we neutralized the situation. We gave him multiple warnings and options to stop shooting and come out. When you shoot a cop, you are done. We saved the whole neighborhood. It was the second time this guy had barricaded himself in this kind of a self-created situation and had shot up a neighborhood. The first time he had barricaded himself in a van and the second time he was in his home.

We always used Mother, our armored vehicle. If someone was held hostage with people inside, we could use this vehicle and rescue them. I helped design the new Mother (Mother 2) which crashed through walls and then returned to my district as Captain. But, I would like to elaborate here on Mother 2. I had a great team of people to work with in SWAT. But I decided for my own self that I wanted more background on SWAT, so I flew to Los Angeles on my own dime to learn about it first-hand. L.A. at that time had the SWAT team. I went down to L.A. with new ideas. I started training. I was working out six days a week and I was in the best shape of my life. I studied all major cases related to SWAT. I conditioned my mind and my body for the job. Anytime something went bad I would find ways to solve the incidents. If police were held hostage or a father was holding kids we went in. We did not wait for support. The first to arrive went in. We took our customized designed armor vehicle that would go right thru walls and we used it. The mother 2 was the best armored vehicle in America and we had great men and women who worked as a team designing it. It was essential for me to change the way we hired people in SWAT. I wanted the know-how of all people, all races, all religions to work as a team, a team for betterment.

We got a federal grant, five police and a new motor and new transmission and we were ready to rock! This was how we worked on Mother, I took the same motor that was in a fire truck and built it (I worked side by side with my dad as a mechanic and I had the knowledge) and I had everything redone and I redesigned Mother and it looked like a tank! It was our secret weapon. It was a new armored vehicle and it was something! Like I say, it could crash through and knock down buildings like nothing ever before! We named it Mother 2 because it was different from the first vehicle, the first Mother—it was better! And, it was effective all over the USA. Mother 2 stormed the nation! It was my officers and myself that designed it and we were damn proud. We built it like a tank! It was the best armored vehicle in the US.

SWAT was filled with great energy! I recruited women into SWAT as well as all types of people from all walks of life and the energy was apparent in SWAT. You could feel the energy! It was amazing. People from all races working side by side! I always had my eye out for equality throughout my entire police career and my time in SWAT reflected my approach and all that I stood for as SWAT Commander. I wanted the best for everyone and to have everyone participate. This is how you change a nation! My goal was to make America safe and when I became SWAT Commander, it wasn't just about Cleveland, it was about America. I always made it part of my job to save lives. Yes. This is how you change the world and make it better.

When I was in the police force I saw things in the big picture and to this day, I still see life this way, in the big picture. I was proud when I was told by everyone who knew me in the police force that my abilities were second to none. As a team I had one thing in my mind and that was to change the climate of crime. SWAT was the change. From the fire and ashes of the Watts riots to the super-cop training with SWAT, SWAT worked as the experts they were to perfect their crisis response.

SWAT came from the ruins and ashes of the Watts Riots in Los Angeles in 1967. It arose as an elite law enforcement unit knows as the Special Weapons and Tactics team. They were super-cops with superior weaponry and negotiating skills used strictly to diffuse extreme criminal situations. The success of SWAT has been astronomical! Used for hostage and terrorist situations, I was honored to be SWAT Commander of Cleveland and be part of the develop of the Mother vehicle that has transformed response strategies to keep the country safe.

*My Life Changed
When I Died~*

Luis Cumba

I was headed to this Asian restaurant where I met my friends once a month to chew the fat. We are all a bunch of retired policemen. I must have passed out in the restaurant. I don't know. I don't remember anything. I was told that after I fell in the restaurant that I got up and I went to eat and then I was taken to the hospital and died. I didn't know anything until I woke up three months later. A lot happened to me while I was dead.

Luis Cumba

CHAPTER SIXTEEN

I remember I was at a desk counter in an air terminal trying to buy a ticket for my wife to get on a helicopter with me. I was feeling the thrill of an unlikely destination and I couldn't wait to experience the adventure. I had been standing in line and we were running late. I stared around at the spotless white walls. After a long wait, I got the ticket and soon we were up in a helicopter streaking the sky. It was a high noon sunshiny day and the clouds were white and fluffy. We put on our ear buds and were listening to music. I love music and I could feel the smile on my face. It was too incredible of a feeling to imagine. We were flightseeing and enjoying the sweeping views of Cleveland when, by some sort of signal the chopper dipped and swayed and lifted us off to Philly where my family lives, and we visited them briefly.

The next thing that happened is there were a lot of important people in the hospital. The Chief of Police among them. And I felt his presence throughout my entire experience. I felt him always being with me. And then it all shifted over to me being held captive in the hospital and I am thinking this is where all the missing people in Cleveland are. The hospital began to feel like some secluded cove where all these people being held hostage were losing time together. I wanted to send a note out to all the cops in the world that the historically missing are right here. I wanted to yell out to them that I knew where the dead mysteriously went missing. It was like a scene from a Hollywood movie. I had the answers to the disappearance and we need to be rescued. Someone needs to get us out of here. Was there a trail of blood or had these people just been to expertly kidnapped that they hadn't left a trace? Had they just vanished and been left for dead.

Being a cop, I started to assess my skills. How was I going to survive this? How was I going to get these people out of here? The missing had been found. I couldn't dare make everyone panic more than they already were. The key to the situation was to remain calm. At first, I didn't know that I was being held in the hospital, but then I realized I was being held captive in the hospital. I had been kidnapped! I didn't panic. I would not show any defiance, resistance, anger or contempt. My only hope was to flee so, I tried to escape. I was determined. I would do this. I would flee and bring help back for the others. I had to get out of here.

I was trying to make a run for it and get to the nearest police station and report the fact that they were holding people hostage at the Cleveland Hospital. And then my experience changed, and I became fascinated by a limousine that just seemed to pull up out of nowhere to take me and my wife in it with the Mexican actress and beautiful lady Eva Mendez. She welcomed our arrival. It was as if she expected us. She asked us how we were and gave us both a kiss on the cheek and then whisked us away to a restaurant where I ate something, and I got sick. The nurses that kidnapped me took me back and I remember being marooned out in the ocean and taken to a featherbed on a Japanese island and there was a pulmonary respiratory surgeon and two Japanese nurses, they were making a concoction for me. It was an antibiotic. I told them I had two transplants and asked them how will they find me way out here? The Cleveland Clinic kept coming to me and it was close to the spot where I was marooned. It was peculiar for I had disappeared. I had just vanished.

And then in a whirlwind, I woke up after being dead for three months speaking fluent Japanese (which I never knew) prior to my coma. A Japanese respiratory guy was working on me. I learned that a policeman I worked with came to the hospital every day and was praying for me the whole time. I must have felt his presence (perhaps he was the Police Chief I felt so strongly in my revelation) and my son and ex-wife came every day to see me. But before I awoke, I felt God speak to me and let me know I was coming back because it wasn't my time yet. God let me know that I had a mission and the mission was to tell the world *how great thou art is.*

I had very little brain activity while I was in my coma for three months. Being in the coma affected my nervous system and muscles and my walking was also a little bit of an issue. I atrophied while I was in the coma and learned they had to put a feeding tube in my stomach. I didn't recognize myself. I didn't look anything like I had the day I went to the Asian restaurant to have lunch with my friends. I had passed out but really, I had entered a coma and come out on the other side. I had gone well beyond the coma.

And as for the feather bed I was on out on some reclusive Japanese island, well I read that if you have revelations that contain a featherbed, it means you will be lifted. And I felt from my experience that God lifted me from my life and lifted me up into a completely changed self, a better self. I became a person who smiles a lot more and is a lot more outgoing and friendlier and a person who gives compliments easily to others. God raised me above my expectations and practices and broadened my personality and my horizons with humor and unconditional love!

When I was in that helicopter, I felt God lift me up and I awoke from my coma with God in my heart even stronger than ever before. To this day, I wonder if God was, indeed, that helicopter that lifted me up and whisked me off across my life and sent me back to earth landing me in one giant hug!

I came back to the world
With the lightness of a cloud~

Luis Cumba

CHAPTER SEVENTEEN

It was as if I was caught in a never-ending mural of youth and everyone on earth had been painted young. There was no wrinkled skin, no one was bald, no one was grey. Everyone was young and exuberant. There were no age spots or bags under anyone's eyes. Everyone's got a perfection complexion. I saw no age. After I got out of my coma, no one looked old. Age was gone. Everything was brand new and shiny and people all looked young and sounded young and I went around complimenting the world on how beautiful it looked! It was like I was in this indescribable dimension and I went around complimenting everyone. I would really compliment the ladies and tell them how beautiful they looked. Maybe I was also seeing the best side of me. I don't know.

It has been said that the coma or being in a coma is one of the most baffling medical conditions in the world. It is the craziest place for God to come to you, but I am sure that God did come to me in my coma. No doubt. But crazier than the coma is what happened to me afterwards. After the coma, I saw everyone young. I felt as if I knew the centuries and they even kept getting younger. It is hard to explain, but it was like I had come back to earth and just stopped at youth. I only saw life as new and young and exciting. No one looked old. I think age reduces the experience of life anyway and this seemed to be more pronounced after my coma. It was weird and wonderful at the same time. It was as if I had entered another reality and this other reality really became the cornerstone of my life. It changed me unbelievably.

Everyone looked young and beautiful even if they were old. I did not see age. I complimented women all the time on their outfits, their make up and overall the way they looked. Their skin was so beautiful, and I kept smiling all the time at everyone. This is very interesting because when I was younger I was an introvert and I didn't smile very often. I wasn't very friendly either. And I rarely said hello to strangers. After my coma, I have this high sensitivity for other people. I am friendly. I go up to people and make people laugh. I really care about everyone and I think that my death discerned the beginning of a new introspectiveness and a deepened spirituality that has me seeing people as truly beautiful! Can you imagine living a life where there is no such thing as age?

I started thinking what kind of elixir have I consumed for people to look like this? When I died did I take some special potion? It was just dying that did it is all is the only thing that I can come up with. After I died and came back to life I was filled with the most inspiring views of everything and everyone. Now I must say that this caused me some puzzlement. But, I began to think that I have been introduced to the extraordinary. Dying, of course, had an emotional impact on me and it woke me up to the beautiful.

Perhaps God felt that seeing everyone young and beautiful would be healing for me. Perhaps God has created the good side of the earth for me to see and associate with and wants me to see the beautiful. I don't know. I haven't figured it all out. But I do know, I am happy, and I live in my heart and in the deepest part of my soul and my fit in life is seeing everything and everybody as young and beautiful to this day. What can I say? I live in the feeling of life and it is wonderful!

And so, not only does everyone look young, something else unbelievable has emerged from my coma. I came out of my coma as a perfect encyclopedia of information. I have remembered everything I have ever learned and ever read since I was a little boy. I had taken a strong fancy to education and it was all coming out after my coma. And so, what happened was all so astounding. I became an authority of the United States Constitution and I came out of my coma speaking fluent Japanese (my respiratory therapist who was attending to me at the time was Japanese).

So much happened to me after I was dead. It seemed as if I came back to life with the lightness of a cloud! Smiling warmly at the world, my personality was friendlier, and my gait was happy! I was gregarious, and it was as if my entire soul and spirit changed. I went up to people. I wasn't shy anymore. It was really something! I didn't recognize myself and my family couldn't even believe that it was me.

But my bubble started breaking~

Luis Cumba

CHAPTER EIGHTEEN

And so, my bubble started breaking~

I remember Cleveland's rate of kid crack-related emergency room admissions was a nightmare and it bothered me. As a cop in all my ranks I worked the streets. I remember we didn't take any breaks. I was out on the streets with my brothers and sisters in blue. I was with them when we crashed into offices to arrest drug dealers. I was out there on the streets trying to dismantle Cleveland's deeply entrenched drug lords and break up the cartel-supplying drugs gangs. I never stayed behind the desk even in all my promotions. As I have mentioned, it wasn't my style. And so, in the process of trying to combat the drug war, participating in the drug raids and dealing with the drug shooting up public, I must have had a cut on one of my fingers or something and that's how I got it, hepatitis C.

I would learn later my fingers were loaded with cuts. I would fix my own cars all the time, just like my dad did. It was a hobby of mine that carried over from my high school mechanic days when my dad taught me everything he knew about fixing cars and trucks and as a downside to it, my fingers were cut. In any case, I remember we got a call from a male committing suicide, so we responded. Now, I had been a medic prior when I was a firefighter and so I was the appropriate person to try to stop the blood. This was back in the late 70's and 80's and no gloves were required. The man had hepatitis (through shooting up with infected needles) and through blood exposure, I contracted hepatitis C. It is spread by blood contamination and you don't get any symptoms, typically from it for years after the exposure. It hit me six years later when the virus attacked my liver leading to inflammation and the doctors told me I needed a liver transplant. I was thirty-three years old when I got exposed.

In 1989 hepatitis C was identified. Widespread screening of the blood supply for hepatitis C began in 1992. It was a long journey from discovery to cure. I was right in the middle of America's hepatitis C journey. I tried treatment after treatment but none of them worked. When I was told I needed a liver transplant, I was filled with a lot of different thoughts. Of course, I was worried about my future, but it made me think about my life and understanding time and things like that. I knew first on the list was the liver transplant and then the kidney transplant. First was the liver and then was the kidney. Hepatitis C also affects the kidney and I started thinking again, even more, about my relationship with time and how things were going to work out for me. It really got me thinking about things.

I had different treatments, and nothing worked. And then, in 2009, I was diagnosed with a mass in my liver and, well, that made things even worse. I was on another level of it all. And then in June 2010, after going through four days of tests making sure everything was functioning I got the okay I could get a transplant and because of the tumor in my liver it elevated my status. July 2010, I was number one on the list for a liver transplant. My blood type was AB negative. This is a very rare blood type. Come September Labor Day I got a call at around 9 or 10 thirty from the Cleveland Hospital and they told me I needed to get there in one hour. I had my bag ready.

Now, around this time, I was in charge of Internal Affairs at the Cleveland police department. They needed to take over when I was in surgery. Everything had to go perfectly. I notified my family and headed down to the clinic. My brother Martin drove in from Pittsburg and my sister Margie from Cleveland went with me. I was prepared for the liver transplant and at 3am a Japanese doctor doing the transplant told my family that there was a great possibility that I could die during this transplant. It was a surgery that could kill me. It was a life-threatening surgery. I survived. I learned later that the organ donor was a young man who had died in a motorcycle accident. I found out he was a plumber and had a wife and children. The family chose to be anonymous and I couldn't get in touch with them to thank them. If by chance, they are reading my book, I want to thank them now.

Right after I got my liver transplant they developed a drug called Harvoni. It was and is a prescription medicine used to treat adults with chronic hepatitis C. It is a combination of ledipasvir and sofosbuvir. Cure rates are about 94 percent to 99 percent. I had no side effects and three months later I was totally free from Hep C and still am. There is no sign of the disease in my system, anywhere. I got my life back and came out of it and got strong again and had absolutely no problems. I went back to work.

It is almost unheard of for someone to get a liver transplant and five months later be back at work! But I am happy to say that it is what happened! I can't believe how smoothly it went. In 2010 the doctors treated the tumor in my liver and placed me on the liver transplant list. I got the transplant in September and in February (five months later) I went back to work. Soon thereafter, I am proud to say I received The Medic Award and Everyday Hero Award! Some people would have retired with on duty exposure compensation, but I went back to work. On Feb 20, 2011, I was back at working doing what I most loved in my life, law enforcement and life was good!

My bubble started bursting in 2012 when I was diagnosed with kidney failure. When I woke up I learned my kidney was not functioning correctly. It was yet another result from Hep C and the initial exposure. At the beginning of 2013 I was blowing up. My legs and chest and body blew up. I couldn't get rid of the water. They put a catheter in my heart to start dialysis. Valentine's day 2013, I started dialysis. They took muscle and water out of me. I was suffering and my son Luis Jr., saw this. And my son couldn't take me suffering and being so weak. And so, on a cold February day (February 24th to be precise) in Cleveland, a blustery day but no snow, I received my kidney transplant. I was in my early 50's and Luis Jr. my son was in his 30's.

Luis Jr. on his own, decided to give me one of his kidneys and give me life. There were a lot of volunteers in my family and I never asked anyone. My son knew the risks, but he told anyone who asked him that I meant the world to him. He was in his thirties and he had a perfect kidney and same blood type as me. He went through the testing. My youngest sister volunteered to give me a kidney. Luis was a perfect match. Feb 2014, I went in for a kidney transplant. They checked me with my son's kidney and he was right next to me. They had to take his kidney out and put it in me. It functioned immediately. We were both fine and still are. This kidney transplant and the love that surrounded it initiated my immersion into Captain Bionic. My son and I both have one kidney. My son is my hero. I remember when we first saw one another after the transplant, it was like every time we see each other. We gave each other a kiss on the cheek and we both said I love you to one another. It was just like any other day.

Today, he lives with me and helps me at home. Not only is he my son and my hero, he is my best friend. Luis, I love you.

THE WILL OF THE PEOPLE OF AMERICA

The long shadow of color has loomed over the United States of America like a black cloud. No two people will ever be sensitive to multicultural issues in the same way. Images of Native Americans, African Americans, Asian Americans, Hispanic Americans and Jewish Americans and women and so on creates enormous problems for America and the will of the people. As a leading authority on civil rights I worked IN the Cleveland Police Department to increase the number of minorities added into the department and redressed issues of racial inequality and I didn't stop there. I have taken the issue of racial hate on the road and have introduced racial love and harmony through my music, handshaking and right here in the pages of my book.

Luis Cumba

EPILOGUE

I have soared in life.

I have vanished in strings of accidental homicides, shake downs, shoplifting busts and drug tailing. I have run after the silver the thugs stole, trailed the kidnappers as well as landed in a coma, died and became Captain Bionic. I have served with the first responders. I was a quiet sensitive kid from Puerto Rico who also grew up to protect the Presidents of America and roll along with their motorcades. Who knew I would grow up to help protect US Presidents against the bad guys in this high-profile procession.

I have been part of the fascinating caravan of sleek dark odd intimidating vehicles and their waving flags that line the roads protecting American Presidents. Intricately protecting the president and his entourage, I rumbled along with the best of them, this one-time quiet sensitive kid from Puerto Rico who always seemed to have an eye for humankind riding along in the Presidential motorcade to protect a few presidents. The presidential motorcade is a symbol of America's might and has always been a source of attention and grandeur when it rumbles the streets. No doubt, the presidential motorcade commands attention from all!

Who would ever think that this sensitive kid from Puerto Rico would grow up and be part of the amazing motorcade anatomy protecting President Ronald Reagan, President Bill Clinton, President George Bush and his son President George W and President Barak Obama? Part of the mission to offer The White House and The Secret Service presidential transport protection in any number of emergencies on behalf of SWAT or the traffic unit, I rolled along with the fleet of armored vehicles, on many occasions, that composed the Presidential Motorcade. Our goal was to keep the President safe. Every threat motivates the motorcade still today and those riding along in it must be prepared that anything could happen.

Ready to meet all emergencies, at the cost of our own lives the motorcade protects the President of The United States. The route is gamed out ahead of time. Chokepoints, shortcuts and threats, real or imagined are considered ahead of time including if the sun is going to be a problem shining in someone's eyes. Once the barricade moves forward it keeps going and no one gets into the route. Riding along in the motorcade to President Ronald Reagan, President Bill Clinton, President George Bush and his son President George W and President Barak Obama remains a big part of my life along with my other big achievement which was working with cops and kids for thirty years and providing the needy with gifts, food and an array of their needs. These experiences have remained a very big part of my life.

I want to reiterate that my dreams made me feel courageous. I did not like the feeling of fear. If an alarm sounded I would want to check it out. If a car plummeted down an embankment and was embedded in a circle of red flashing lights, I wanted to be the fireman or the policeman to disengage someone from the wreckage. I wanted to rescue people. I wanted to be that guy who was not afraid to jump in. It didn't matter if it was someone darting from an alley screaming for help or if I was running a sick feverish friend to a clinic I wanted to make it all right and be a first line responder to disaster situations. I was quick on my feet and a fast runner and ready to help. I wanted to help. I wanted to make things better. I have always been the type of person who says, *what am I going to give, not what am I going to get.* And this is what makes me who I am, this and my God.

I've seen a lot in my career as a police officer. I've experienced the fast-talking con-artists, thugs eager to take lives for the hell of it, protected the iron walls of safes, the innocent from the counter-snatchers, pocket-pickers, daring robbers and the neat-handed pilferers and the confident tricksters who pretend to be your friend, rob you and try to cultivate a society of unpardonable breaches of trust. The sheer ingenuity of criminals is infinite and always on the loose. A thug's creative inventiveness and reckless audacity and schemes for escaping penalties mind boggling.

I've seen first responders risk their lives every day to save lives every day. I was a proud first responder and every day I am proud of the first responders and my brothers and sisters in blue who wake up to save the world and help those in need. I have been given something unbelievable, a second chance at life. And, I have emerged from my coma as a perfect encyclopedia of information of everything I have ever learned! God has blessed me with good humor and personality and a spirit that never, for a moment, has failed me under any circumstances. I have remembered everything I have ever learned and ever read since I was a little boy. I had taken a strong fancy to education as a youngster and it was all coming out from my coma experience. Dying has made me live like I have never lived before!

All I can say is my life has been astounding. Every part of my life has been astounding! After my coma I became an authority of the United States Constitution and I came out of my coma speaking fluent Japanese (the pulmonary professional attending to me was Japanese when I awoke, and I awoke speaking Japanese—it is truly amazing!). I remember everything I have ever learned resulting from my coma. I died and through my coma God gave me the power to be everything I can be. And so, I have written my life story and shot a rocket into literature with all that has happened to me in my life and death. By writing my book I have tried to do something for the causes in which I believe and the situations for which I oppose. Poverty, inequality, suffering, bigotry and oppression all need to be stamped out along with war and violence. It can all be changed. It can all be made better. I have said this over and over and will continue to do so.

I have lived and learned. When life's challenges faced me, I faced them back, square in the eye and still do. I don't run away from challenges. I challenge challenges and I have done my best in this memoir to capture the truth of my life, along with my emotions, and offer insight, inspiration and wisdom to those who read my story. I have told my story to the best of my ability. Authenticity has not just been important and essential in my pages but in my life. Authenticity in life is essential. Being who you really are is essential.

My friends and colleagues and family have always known with me that what you see in what you get. I am, indeed fortunate, to have had the guidance of great and wonderful people. The support of my family has picked me up in life and who I am is all due to God. Yes! God has provided me with strength and wisdom and a comic perspective that has allowed me to face my challenges and my elements of trauma with a healthy light perspective filled with humor.

I had to die for a while to get where I am today. My strong affinity with God has always been present but when I was dead it really came through. I realized, too, that it is not an all-about-me demeanor that makes someone a good person. It doesn't give us the perspective we need to make society better. It doesn't even furnish us with the acceptance and competence to make ourselves better. A selfish perspective on life is what makes us short sighted and doesn't make us better people which in the end is what it is all about. Trust me on this. It is about being a good person and being kind to others. Don't allow yourself to be modified by events in life. Remain kind and attentive to all living things, the elderly, animals, the flowers!

I excelled under unlikely circumstances. I turned over a new leaf while I was dead. I became more outgoing with a genuine concern for humankind. I compliment people now, I try to say nice things to change someone's day for the better. I am passionate about kindness and compassion, although I have always had that in me, but it was really brought out after my coma. After my coma, I seemed to remember everything that I have ever learned, and I think that is for a reason. We are supposed to share wisdom and through the sharing of wisdom we will gain insight and knowledge and revel in being better people.

My memoir has been written toward the close of a busy life. I have always had an eye off in the distance. Always thinking about the future, I remember stepping quickly along the streets of Cleveland wearing a warm winter coat buttoned all the way up close to my chin to keep the cold out. I remember that I always had this quick gait to me. I was popular. People loved me. They loved me, but I was a shy stranger in their lives. I always was on the shy side. But after my death, I am not shy anymore. I am friendly and outgoing!

I guess death does that to you! Some inimitable force and elegance of style seemed to take over me when I returned to life and I always find myself today, smiling a lot more and easily getting into conversations with people and giving compliments to everyone! Women have always been a delight to my eyes but today I am a lot more social. I am gregarious and easily attempt a conversation! I never did this before I died. So, I guess I can say that death has done a lot for me I life including making me a great scholar, in the highest sense of the term. I really do think that in death, I must have studied life! I am sure of it! Since I have died, I have returned to life breathing as quite a different man.

My early experiences in life were sensitive ones. I believe I was overly sensitive before I died but didn't know how to show it. I was wrapped up in my career and working out, being in great shape. I was very involved in my career in law enforcement and moving up the ranks every step I could in law enforcement. Have been ambitious since I was two years old! In my life I have meandered through the pages of so many books and studied like there was no tomorrow so much information, so I could get ahead in my career and when I emerged from my coma I remembered everything I've ever read.

Later in life, after my death, I became mesmerized by the tranquility of the water and found beauty in the setting sunsets which changed my heart. I found time to take the sunsets in and enjoy them. When I was working I didn't have the time. It is a regret of mine. I should have made the time because in the end in the realities of life, death and experience, it is what it is all about. Today, I make time to look at myself between my beliefs and realize that other people have beliefs and opinions and I must be open to those beliefs as well. The only way for there to be change is to have hope and the only way for hope, is to be able to listen to the beliefs of others. I have always been for the people and their struggles for life, liberty and better living conditions. I will always stand for this. It is my vision for life.

And now, at the close of this book I feel as if I have emerged from the dust and the smoke of hard-fought political battles and the unceasing struggle for respect and social value changes because I have lived in the spirit of life. I have lived in the spirit of cities and towns. I have felt exuberance, experience and expectation. I have felt the outlooks of millions and the sadness and brilliance of those struggling to elicit their views and opinions. I know because I was one of them.

It is about transforming the lives of communities. It is all about people recognizing people and their importance in society. It was so natural that me, Luis Cumba and my character along with my constant overwork and passion should lead me to be so passionate and protective of the frailties of others. Perhaps, the most beautiful trait in my dichotomy is the light that was planted at my feet when I came back from being dead. It has made me want to sing and play my bass all the time and smile! And dear reader, if you noticed that love is sprinkled throughout my pages don't look at it as me being redundant. It was intended that way! I hope I have just made you smile!

I have attempted to uncover the unseen in this book and through my pages allow my readers to accompany me as I recall the painful things and the historical wounds that have made up my life. I have tried very hard to analyze myself throughout this writing journey to determine why my past at times is so difficult to understand. As a historian, I see no better place to start understanding history and its importance but in my very own pages. Still and all, my time travel to death and back doesn't have an exact explanation except to let everyone know *how great thou art is*—how great God is! God sees everything. Be kind to all. Be compassionate to all. Projecting pain to anything or anyone is a great personal loss. Many decades later, I still recall how I helped my grandfather in Puerto Rico guide the oxen with a twig. I hope that I didn't hurt them.

I hope you have enjoyed reading my book! Keep the faith and stay positive and stay close to God. If you do that, you will be okay. Clarify your role in life. Live life with gusto, and please keep the search going for happiness. This is all just another step on the road to being okay. And as for me, I will continue to face my challenges and continue my fight for life, liberty and safety for all. And every day, I will continue to search deeply for what it means to be human and pray that racism ends in my life time.

Tomorrow can be different.
Thanks for reading.

Luis Cumba

CAPTAIN BIONIC

POST EPILOGUE:

FROM THE DESK OF LUIS CUMBA

LUIS CUMBA'S TACO RECIPE

Taco recipe, one pound of ground meat; gather garlic, cilantro, sweet pepper, adobo sold in most stores, mixture of salt, pepper garlic, and onions. Chop and ground in blender. Add mixture to ground meat and cook add water and taco sauce and cook for five minutes. Put on shells/ add hot sauce to liking.

LUIS CUMBA'S CHICKEN RECIPE

Yellow rice and chicken. 1 cup of rice add water and the mixture I used for taco, no hot sauce. Add oil and salt and pack of sazon found in most stores, coloring. Cook chicken in pot ¾ of way. Bring water to boil with rice add spices mixture, adobo, sazon and add chicken bring to boil. When water is vaporized, simmer and add cover to steam and dry rice—eat and enjoy!

LUIS CUMBA'S BLESSINGS

Friendship is part of my spiritual journey.
And God is a big part of this journey.

Luis Cumba

God has shown me the path of being kind and patient.
God has helped me to walk this path and be easy on myself and on others.

Luis Cumba

On Sundays, I am with my God.
I find myself to be very happy on Sundays.

Luis Cumba

We would go in immediately to save someone. We wouldn't wait. Burning
building, kidnapping, domestic violence, first responders go in!
That is what first responders do. First responders try to save lives~

Luis Cumba

*I don't know who you are. I don't know what you believe. It doesn't matter.
My job is to save your life. This is a first responder's thinking.*

Luis Cumba

*Put yourself in a first responder's shoes
And you may find it will scare the living daylights out of you.*

Luis Cumba

*I sometimes leap from tall buildings
Jump from roofs
Run faster than a speeding bullet
But, I am not superman
I am a police officer*

Luis Cumba

*Communities need to know
We survive not as one, but as millions…together~*

Luis Cumba

*My mother stole my heart
The day she taught me not to steal~*

Luis Cumba

CPSIA information can be obtained
at www.ICGtesting.com
Printed in the USA
BVHW091537150419

545536BV00012B/866/P

9 780960 088119